D0230894

1 2 JUN 2022

SWIMMING TEACHING AND COACHING

LEVEL I

COLLEGE OF RIPON
AND YORK ST. JOHN
YORK CAMPUS
LIBRARY

EDITED BY RICK CROSS

Published by ASA Swimming Enterprises Ltd
1991

York St. John College

3 8025 00492970 2

The Amateur Swimming Association
Harold Fern House
Derby Square
Loughborough
Leicestershire LE11 0AL
Telephone: (01509) 230431 Fax: (01509) 610720

All rights reserved. No part of this publication may be reproduced or transmitted in any form or by any means, electronic or mechanical, including photocopying, recording or any information storage and retrieval system now known or to be invented without permission in writing from the publisher.

First published 1991
Reprinted 1992, 1994, 1995
Copyright © ASA, 1991
ISBN 0 900052 19 8

Editor: Rick Cross
Illustration: Peter Cullen
Cover design: David Allton
Designed by: Rick Cross
Printed by: Echo Press Ltd, Loughborough

Wherever the pronoun "he" has been used it should be interpreted as applying equally to men and women as appropriate.

Contents

Preface

The predecessor to this book, *The Teaching of Swimming,* published by the Amateur Swimming Association (ASA), ran through 15 editions. In the intervening years general increases in the knowledge of swimming and teaching/coaching have considerably changed the expectations and challenges of those involved. With this in mind, the ASA decided to commission two new publications. This first book is intended to span the material appropriate to the earlier levels of teaching/coaching, whilst the second book will take up issues in much greater depth and at a higher level. Clearly, the basic ingredient of any book of this nature, no matter at what level, is to improve the quality of teaching/coaching and, thereby, bring about an improvement in the performance of those who are being taught/coached.

The ASA decision to commission this series of books has also produced a subtle, but important, outcome. This book embraces the concept of a more unified teaching/coaching "profession". The teacher/coach roles frequently overlap, as does the need for their skills. Some national governing bodies of sport do not have this dilemma and call everyone concerned by a single title. Throughout this book an attempt has been made to bridge the gap by referring to "teacher/coach" or "teaching/coaching". George Bernard Shaw has often been misquoted, and we must surely try to avoid future attitudes polarising into:

Either

Those who can – DO
Those who can't – TEACH
Those who cannot do either – COACH!

or

Vice versa

The most important point is that swimmers need different kinds of help at different times and levels of their career in the sport.

Ideally, those with less experience in teaching/coaching should be working under supervision and getting guidance from more experienced and qualified colleagues. If swimmers, at all levels, are to get the best help, teachers/coaches should make every effort to increase their own backgrounds in the many aspects of the sport. This can be done by attending courses and by seeking more information from the wide range of literature available. Part V of this book, *Additional Information,* provides a good basis for those who do decide to investigate matters further.

The paramount feature of any swimming programme should be safety. Chapter 5 makes reference to this in some detail. It is important, not only morally, but also because of the demands of the Health and Safety Commission, that everyone concerned with poolside activities should be familiar with safety procedures. The ASA strongly urges that all concerned with poolside activities should seriously consider taking the joint ASA/RLSS Lifesaving Certificate, designed specifically for teachers/coaches, or other RLSS awards.

Rick Cross
Editor

Rick Cross

Qualified at Loughborough. Taught in a wide range of schools before becoming an LEA adviser and later a head of teaching studies and in service education in higher education. He is now a freelance lecturer/ consultant in education and recreation. Rick is also a member of several ASA and ISTC committees, including being Chairman of the Joint ASA/ISTC Working Party reviewing ASA qualifications in preparation for the introduction of National Vocational Qualifications. He is also an ASA Principal Tutor. Editor/author of two books on swimming.

Introduction

The structure of swimming in Great Britain

Trevor Thomas

Swimming, in all its disciplines, is organised in England, Scotland and Wales, the three "home" countries, as the **Amateur Swimming Federation of Great Britain (ASFGB).** The Federation is affiliated to the world governing body of swimming, **Federation Internationale de Natation Amateur, (FINA).** FINA is responsible for the control of all swimming events at the World Championships, Olympic Games and the major regional events between FINA member countries. The ASFGB also affiliates to the **Ligue Europeene de Natation (LEN)** so that its members can compete in the European Championships, the major event in our region. For swimming purposes, Northern Ireland (Ulster) combines with Eire to form the Irish ASA, and affiliates to FINA as a member country and governing body in its own right. The three "home" countries also have their own governing bodies, the Amateur Swimming Association of England (ASA), the Scottish Amateur Association (SASA) and the Welsh Amateur Swimming Association (WASA). They control their own domestic swimming programmes and take part in "friendly" international competition, including the Commonwealth Games, in which they each compete as a "Sport Country".

The objects of all three home Associations are the same:
- to promote the teaching and practice of swimming, diving, synchronised swimming and water polo and stimulate public opinion in favour of providing proper accommodation and facilities for these disciplines.
- to draw up, publish and enforce uniform laws for the control and regulation of amateur participation in all disciplines, and to deal with any infringement thereof.

The Amateur Swimming Association of England, usually simply known as the ASA, was founded in 1869 and is the oldest governing body of swimming in the world. The laws of the Association, along with other policy decisions, are decided at the annual Council Meeting of the ASA which is held in the early part of February each year. The ASA Committee, in accordance with the laws of ASA, has the power to manage the affairs of the Association between Council Meetings. At its first meeting following each Council, the ASA Committee appoints the various specialist Technical Committees which look after the wide range of ASA interests and responsibilities at national level. Currently that range includes:

Diving	Education
Investment	Masters Swimming
Medical Advisory	National Judicial Tribunal
Public Relations	Scientific Advisory
Swimming	Swimming Facilities
Synchronised Swimming	Water Polo

For the general government of the sport the ASA is divided into the Midland, Northern, North-Eastern, Southern and Western Districts. These Associations have similar objects to those of the ASA. Each District is comprised of all the counties, affiliated clubs, local, private and Schools Swimming Associations with headquarters within that District's boundaries. Some Associations are eligible to affiliate direct to the ASA, e.g., the Armed Services and the English Schools' Swimming Association (ESSA). A Club is made up of members and, unless they wish to take part in competition, there is no need for a club to affiliate to the District Association although the majority do so. There are, however, regulations covered in ASA Laws (ASA Handbook) which control the rights of swimmers to take part in certain competitions. Some of these laws are designed to protect young children from excessive competition demands and specify minimum ages for particular events.

The District administrative and technical committee structure is similar to that of the ASA. Its main objective is to implement ASA policy in general at District and at County levels, as well as enforcing the laws, rulings, conditions and resolutions of the ASA. The Districts also promote their own swimming, diving, water-polo and synchronised swimming championships and competitions, as well as national and international events on behalf of the ASA or ASFGB when called upon to do so.

International events fall into two categories, firstly, "friendly" events in which the ASA competes as England. These include the Commonwealth Games, contests against Scotland and Wales, often known as the "Home Country Internationals", and others where contests are arranged between nations by invitation. Examples of this type of match are those arranged for the England Senior, Intermediate and Youth squads. The major contests such as the World Championships, Olympic Games and the LEN (European) Championships, are swum as ASFGB and are the second category of international competitions.

As previously mentioned in the list of specialist Technical Committees there is, in the context of this publication, one committee worthy of special mention, i.e., the Education Committee. It is responsible for the production of swimming publications, books, films and other educational matter published in the name of the ASA. The Education Committee is also responsible for initiating and introducing the ASA Awards Scheme designed as a sound educational base with a logical progression from earliest stages to specialist disciplines. The ASA Proficiency Awards in swimming range from swimming 5 metres with/without a buoyancy aid through to the Ultimate Swimmer award. There are Water Skill Awards, Challenge Awards, and awards for Personal Survival and speed swimming. There are also awards giving opportunities to encourage progress in Diving, Water Polo and Synchronised Swimming by introducing and developing the basic skills required for each of those disciplines.

Learning to swim can commence at any age, from the very young baby to the adult of "mature" years. It often commences during the informal family recreational sessions and/or a programmed parent and child classes organised by the Local Authority or the local swimming club. For the majority of non-swimmers more formal learning takes place after the age of five or six years, when children start school. Sadly, fluctuations in the economic climate are frequently reflected in the reduction of school swimming lessons. Parents, therefore, often have to look for alternative sources for lessons. These can be found in a local swimming club, Local Authority classes, Community Colleges or lessons at a "Swim School" in a privately owned or hired facility. Information on the availability of such classes can be found at the local pool, Citizen Advice Bureau, the local library and from advertisements in the local paper or the 'Yellow Pages'.

The best way to learn to swim is to enrol for a block of regular lessons. The duration of the lesson can vary between 20 to 30 minutes dependent on the age and ability of the pupil. The number of lessons can also vary, from the one lesson per week over a ten or twelve week period to a block of lessons scheduled to be completed within a shorter period of time. The latter is considered to be the best option, two lessons per week is better than one, and ten lessons spread over two weeks is preferable to ten lessons spread over ten weeks. This ideal option is not readily available but practice between formal lessons is to be encouraged. In every case, however, the customer is advised to ascertain the quality of the teaching/coaching on offer by ensuring that staff hold an appropriate qualification, such as one of the ASA Teaching/Coaching Certificates. As the skills and confidence in strokes evolves other skills can be introduced as an introduction to the other swimming disciplines. If not already a member of a swimming club the way forward to excellence is to join a club that specialises in the teaching/coaching of the discipline of your choice. Some clubs include several disciplines in their activities, whilst others might only be active in one field.

As indicated earlier the ASA has a wide range of interests. It is linked with companies such as, **Swimming Times Ltd,** which publishes a monthly magazine of the same name, **Swimming Enterprises Ltd,** the commercial arm of the Association, and the **Institute of Swimming Teachers & Coaches (ISTC).** The Institute currently has more than 10,000 members and has representation on every ASA Technical Committee. It works very closely with the governing body, particularly in the field of education and training of teachers/coaches. The ASA also has links with a number of independent bodies involved in the world of aquatics, e.g., the English Schools Swimming Association (ESSA), the Royal Life Saving Society (RLSS) and the British Swimming Coaches Association (BSCA), and there are Joint Consultative Committees with each of these independent groups. The Joint Consultative Committees meet regularly to discuss matters of mutual interest such as safety in swimming pools, education, publications, joint awards, government policies and their possible impact on the sport, etc.

From the above brief review it will be seen that there is more to the sport of swimming than just "swimming". It is broad in its nature, and so are the ramifications of managing it. However, it is always useful to be reminded that the prime object of the ASA is:

"To promote the teaching and practice of swimming, diving, synchronised swimming and water polo..."
(ASA Handbook, 1990)

In other words, people in the water matter most.

PART I

TEACHING/COACHING

ITS IMPLICATIONS

Introduction to Part I

Most people can float, and by the introduction of appropriate limb actions they learn to swim. Reasons for learning to swim might differ from person to person, but generally they fall under the following headings:

Survival
- **personal** – the ability to save one's own life and possibly reduce the need for others to risk their lives
- **life saving** – to have the ability to train in order to save somebody else's life in an emergency

Fitness
- **exercise** – as a means of providing the opportunities for experiencing the benefits of regular exercise

Recreation
- **social** – as a means of bringing new friends through membership of a club
  - the activity can be enjoyed with one or more friends, i.e., a "team" is not necessary
  - family participation of all ages and abilities is possible
- **economic** – costs are minimal for equipment
  - other costs are comparatively low
- **leisure** – it is a means of allowing safer access to other water based pursuits, e.g., sailing

Therapy
- **people with disabilities** – water is supportive and reduces the stress normally brought on by other weight bearing activities
- **freedom of movement** – activities can be undertaken without the need for great strength

Competition
- **personal interests** – the ability to swim enables an individual to compete in a wide range of activities in the four disciplines of diving, swimming, synchronised swimming and water polo
- **personal achievement** – competition can also be in the form of the challenges and tests offered by the ASA Awards Schemes

Part I, therefore, is designed to introduce the reader to some of the background to the process of being a teacher/coach.

Chapter 1

Considerations for teaching/coaching and learning

Rick Cross

Introduction

Theory versus practice

For many teachers/coaches the mere mention of the word "theory" makes them wince. "Never mind the theory", they say, "Get on with the practical – that's where it counts". Whilst some sympathy might be extended to those with such feelings, it should be remembered that there is a strong relationship between good practice and knowledge of its underpinning theory. A sound understanding of theoretical principles helps to create the **thinking** teacher/coach with an ability to make sound judgements and decisions in a wide variety of situations. Non-thinking teachers/coaches might be limited by the lack of flexibility of approach needed to overcome a wide variety of problems arising from the unusual situations in which they are placed. No one book or course, no matter how long or good, can hope to provide the experience of every situation likely to be met in teaching/coaching. The application of principles, therefore, provides the tools to enable teachers/coaches think their way through many of the situations in which they can find themselves.

We teach/coach **people,** not swimming. One of the problems about teaching/coaching is that learners learn at different rates and for different reasons. So, apart from the passing on of knowledge of swimming, there is also the matter of knowledge of human relationships. Because we are human, we all have individual responses to both the teacher/coach and the learning process. Good teachers/coaches have a variety of resources at their disposal and knowledge of people, and how they learn, **must** figure in their background. Teachers/coaches get excited because the learner gets it right and, sometimes, frustration strikes because learning is not occurring. Either way, the teacher/coach must continually ask himself, **"Why?"** Answering that question provides the basis for future progress. Failure to question one's self will lead to self satisfaction, complacency and dull, repetitious teaching/coaching. The learners deserve better than that – no matter whether they are non-swimmers or Olympic Champions.

Teaching/coaching – is there a difference?

Those with some teaching/coaching experience in swimming will know that, unlike some other sporting activities, there is a differentiation between teaching and coaching. In the view of some it is a matter of status. This is unfortunate since the sport needs both and, in reality, they need each other. It is a matter of roles and tasks since international swimmers start out as non-swimmers and frequently the work of teachers and coaches overlaps. Both are setting out to improve the quality of their learners' performances in the water, whether at the non-swimmer or the international level, by whatever means are appropriate to that level.

What is good teaching/coaching?

One test of the success of a teacher/coach might be, "Have the learners, at whatever level, improved their performance as a result of the teacher/coach?" Did the non-swimmer cover his first five metres, or did the Olympic swimmer win and/or break a record? Such a test fails to take into account the methods employed by the teacher/coach to bring about the improvements, i.e., did the outcome, regardless of the cost in human terms, take priority over everything else? The good teacher/coach is going to give serious consideration to not only the outcome, but also the process which their performer experiences. Public humiliation, for example, "You are the only one in the class who cannot swim!" or "I know you have just done a personal best time, but it's not good enough!", by a teacher/coach might produce short term improvements in performance, but long term such an approach might well cause serious personal stress, particularly for the young, even to the extent of giving up the sport.

The good teacher/coach, therefore, will try to understand the needs of the individuals with whom they are working, and adapt their approach accordingly. Effective teaching/coaching means that realistic outcomes are established for the learner and that there is a good match between the task and the ability/needs of the learner so that the outcomes are achieved. The good teacher/coach will attempt not only to improve the quality of the learners' performances, but also their knowledge and understanding of what they are doing. Explanations will be given of not only **what** is to be done, but also **why** it is being done, bearing in mind each individual learner's level of understanding.

Teaching and Learning

The individual and what makes the difference

Individuals differ in many ways:

- physically
- intelligence
- sociability
- psychologically
- socially and social groups
- sex
- maturation rate
- age
- innate ability
- previous experience
- motivation

Chapter two will deal in more detail with the influences of these factors. Loosely, all these aspects of being different might be described as learner variables. This rather daunting list becomes even more formidable when one considers the possible combinations of the above when various groups are formed – and to which must be added, of course, the impact of the teacher/coach with his own list of "differences". The teacher/coach has, therefore, to take into account a whole range of individual differences which will influence the group/class response to the work and tasks being set. Watering a flower bed with a watering can makes all the flowers wet to a greater or lesser extent, but did those which needed more or less water get what they needed? Pouring information/knowledge over a group of human beings leaves a similar question about needs and their fulfilment unanswered. The amount each individual learns will be greatly influenced by his own set of individual differences. Certainly, individuals collectively form groups/classes, and will have some general similarities in their strengths and weaknesses, and which might be a feature of the group. However, that will not reduce the need for the teacher/coach to provide individual attention.

Management and organisation

Effective management, i.e., having control over the learners, their environment, experiences and organisation, is an important feature of the role of teacher/coach. The basis of the groupings of various individuals within the class should be carefully considered. Groupings, for example, might be made on the basis of:

- endurance
- technical ability
- safety
- previous knowledge/experience
- water depth and individual height
- common strengths or weaknesses
- strokes to be worked
  etc

In other words, groups are based on good, reasoned judgement.

Having established that individuals have different needs within the group, and having also established that groups are formed around common themes, efficient management of groups is frequently based on the use of "Ones" and "Twos" or "A"s and "B"s, often referred to as flight or wave organisation. It is not essential that groups are equal in size since human beings do not fall neatly into this arrangement. Similarly, lanes might be organised by stroke, ability, etc. In the first instance the use of groups simply breaks down the numbers in the class to allow for better use of water space or reduce stress on the swimmers of whatever ability they might be. More to the point, the groupings will be based on ability so that more appropriate techniques or workloads can be developed.

Motivation

Learning is more than the learner being present during the session. The teacher/coach role is to encourage the learner to **want** to learn. Examples of possible ways of doing this are:

- setting goals/achievement levels
- offering praise
- providing feedback, NB praise is not, in itself, feedback
- using a variety of ideas and practices
- using appropriate practices for the level of the group
- using appropriate equipment to provide the level of support required
- demonstrating improvements by showing peer performances
- making sensible use of award/incentive schemes
- using a variety of lesson/session forms from time to time, e.g., orthodox lesson, schedule lesson, time/distance lesson, recreational/fun sessions, lane/chain swimming, schedule session etc
- listening to what the learner has to say; expressing an interest in how they **feel** about what they are doing

● enjoyment and satisfaction; the learning experience of any performer, no matter at what level, should be enjoyable. The nature of the enjoyment will vary from the fun of a non-swimmer playing simple games to the more able performer enjoying a competition or a particular training session because of having won or improved as a result of some very hard work over several months. The nature of the environment and its degree of pleasantness, light, warmth etc, will also feature in the enjoyment factor.

Preparation

Sound preparation is the basis of all good teaching/coaching. It should demonstrate an understanding of the need for progression in both skill demands and workloads. There should be links with both previous and future sessions so that one session is not taken in isolation, but is part of a scheme or programme. The preparatory work will indicate not only WHAT is going to be presented to the group, but also HOW it is going to be developed. It is at this stage, also, that consideration will be given to the way groups are going to be organised and managed. The approach to preparation, therefore, revolves around the following considerations in which the process of **planning, implementation and evaluation** is followed:

● what does the teacher/coach want the learner to learn?
● what activities/practices/drills are needed to assist that learning to occur?
● what organisation and management arrangements are necessary to create the most effective learning environment?
● after the session, carry out an evaluation to see whether learning did occur, and to what extent it occurred for each individual within the group
● decide how that evidence be utilised in the next session.

Effective preparation will provide confidence for the teacher/coach in both the material to be covered and the ability to cover it.

Communication between teacher/coach and the learner

We communicate with each other in three ways:

● **visually** – what we see being done; a demonstration, a video etc
● **verbally** – what is said by the teacher/coach
● **manually** – by the teacher/coach assisting the performer to create the correct patterns of movement

Usually, teachers/coaches combine these methods, e.g., by means of a demonstration (visual) accompanied by an explanation (verbal), or a swimmer's hand is moved through a given path (manual) whilst the teacher/coach explains (verbal) what the swimmer should be feeling and remembering. The latter method is probably the least effective and should be used sparingly. Good communication needs clarity of signal, movement, words etc which, in turn, results from the teacher/coach having clarity of thought and a sound knowledge base from which to select material.

The relationships of the teacher/coach with the groups in their care are key issues if effective learning is to occur. The ability of the teacher/coach to recognise a variety of responses of their groups will influence/modify their approach to the way the work proceeds. The class/group can be alert, enthusiastic, interested on the one hand, or bored, whispering/talking among themselves, or just plain fighting on the other! The cues or signs of responses are both verbal and non-verbal. Verbal cues might come in the way questions are asked or answered by the members of the group. The non-verbal cues might come in the form of eye contact, facial expression, physical movements, e.g., a shrug of the shoulders, or posture in general. The teacher/coach might respond to the group's efforts by means of verbal reinforcement, e.g., "Well done, try...next time", or by non-verbal reinforcement, e.g., by a smile or a nod, although they are often combined. The outcome of this is feedback. This is the basis of providing the performer with information so that the performance can be repeated or modified for subsequent improvements.

The observation of the cues will provide the teacher/coach indications of whether or not learning is occurring for each individual in the group. Failure to recognise the cues will probably mean that the teacher/coach will set inappropriate tasks or workloads, or even use inappropriate language or terminology. A continuation of setting inappropriate activities will lead to boredom, if the tasks are too easy, or frustration if they are too difficult. Either way, the individual's time is being wasted, and this could eventually create discipline and control problems, or even a failure to reappear for subsequent sessions. It must be remembered that **telling** does not necessarily mean that learning has occurred. If it were that simple, teachers/coaches would be out of a job in a very short time!

Obstacles to good communication can often be related to:
- **learner saturation** – being asked to think about too much in too short a time
- **distractions** – noisy or cold environment, spectator (often parent) waving or calling
- **confused presentation of material** – sequencing of activities not progressive and therefore making the learner's task even more difficult
- **wrong assumptions made by the teacher/coach** – the fact that several members of the group seem to understand some teaching/coaching terminology and quickly carry out instructions may lead to some wrong assumptions about every member of the group. Another example of the teacher/coach making the wrong assumptions might be in the matter of group behaviour. Two badly behaved swimmers in a group of 12 might lead the teacher/coach to assume that the whole group is a problem. Care in the interpretation of the cues is essential. Whilst first impressions should not be discounted, a more careful monitoring of the group at work will provide much clearer evidence of the true situation
- **poor teacher/coach image** – just as the teacher/coach has expectations of the group so, too, the group has expectations of the teacher/coach. The general demeanour, appearance, voice, sense of humour and bearing of the teacher/coach will indicate to the group whether or not they are in the charge of a pleasant, confident, competent, knowledgeable person who will have their safety and well being at heart and somebody with whom they would like to work
- **repetitive, unimaginative ideas** – a good teacher/coach will endeavour to reduce learner frustration by providing a variety of ideas on a given theme, but still remember that the young child in particular appreciates the security of repeating an action which has already produced success acknowledged by the teacher/coach. To hastily move on from one idea to another too quickly will greatly reduce the learning rate.

Award and incentive schemes
For many years the ASA has produced encouragement schemes over a wide range of skills and tasks. In doing so it has acknowledged the importance of incentives in the motivation of those who are anxious to improve their skills. Getting an award is not only a matter of a personal achievement of a given standard, it can also provide a public demonstration of that achievement. Whilst some people would view the winning of the badge as sufficient reward, others would feel that the reward was incomplete until it went on show. Some individuals, of course, are so self-motivated that these external (extrinsic) factors are totally unnecessary.

From the teacher/coach point of view the use of incentive schemes should be carefully considered. Whilst there is little doubt that these schemes are incentives for improvements in performance, it is essential that they are used as a means to an end and not made the end itself. Judicious use within a teaching/coaching programme, so that they might be construed as an aid to learning and improving by monitoring progress, is the most effective application of incentive schemes. The frequent and regular use of such schemes, so that they become the be all and end all of the teaching/coaching programme, is not educationally sound. Too frequent use implies that little or no teaching/coaching is taking place and, therefore, by extension, little improvement will occur. An additional important consideration is that teachers/coaches should try to ensure that any individual entered for such an award should have a reasonable chance of gaining it. A series of disastrous failures will do nothing for the self-confidence of the individual performer concerned. Furthermore, it might also imply poor judgement on the part of the teacher/coach. Teachers/coaches should make every effort to familiarise themselves with the nature and range of the ASA award schemes available, so that they can choose those most appropriate to the levels and aspirations of the classes/groups with which they work.

Demonstration and observation

Earlier in this chapter reference was made to the three methods of communication: namely, visual, verbal and manual. Further consideration of these is necessary in relation to the topic of demonstration and observation. The visual image, whether it be in the form of a live performance, video, etc, can have considerable impact on the observers' subsequent attempts to improve their performance, particularly if it is accompanied by a good commentary of points to be noted. Teachers/coaches frequently make use of demonstrations as a means of providing a clearer picture of what is to be attempted. For this to be effective, several points need to be considered:

- **accuracy** – since the point of providing the demonstration is to offer an example of what is needed, it is essential that a demonstration should be **accurate.** The learner is unlikely to be in a position to separate the inaccurate from the accurate
- **choice of demonstrator** – there are several alternatives when making this choice. The teacher/coach might perform the movement on dry land. If this is the case then the movement should be carried out with the body as near to the horizontal plane, i.e., the swimming position, as possible. To expect a performer learning a new movement to interpret a demonstration done in the standing position, i.e., the vertical, into an action which he will be doing in the horizontal plane, is likely to confuse rather than clarify.

  If the teacher/coach chooses a performer to demonstrate in the water, then the impact is likely to be greater if that performer is from within that group. The response of the group is likely to encompass feelings of, "If he can do that, I'll have a go." If there is no single performer in the group capable of providing a **good** demonstration, then perhaps more than one might be able to show what is needed in parts, e.g., one to show leg action, another the arm action and body position. Occasionally, it might be necessary to invite a capable performer from outside the group. Again, level of capability is important in creating a positive response from the observers. If the demonstration is obviously far in advance of the group's current level then it could have an adverse effect on its morale
- **what is to be demonstrated** – the teacher/coach should have a clear idea of precisely **why** the demonstration is being offered, e.g., showing the entry position of the hands in Front Crawl. If necessary, the teacher/coach should have a quiet word with the demonstrator about the precise nature of the performance before it happens, and whilst the class/group is still working on some other activity

- **what is to be said** – some thought should be given at the preparation stage to the points of the demonstration which are to be emphasised by the teacher/coach. The number of points to be made should be limited and clearly stated. Long, involved explanations are counter-productive. The use of question and answer techniques by the teacher/coach is a useful method of checking whether or not the important points have been noted by the group. Encouragement should also be given for the observers to ask questions for clarification of points
- **position of the observers** – careful consideration should be given to the best angles from which the observers can see the demonstration. This will be influenced by what is being emphasised. General body position, for example, would normally be viewed from the side, whilst the width of entry of the hands, or the width of the arm and leg actions of Breaststroke would normally be viewed from head on or from the rear
- **position of the teacher/coach** – the teacher/coach should try to take up a position which will enable both the demonstration and the observers to be seen, e.g., slightly to one side of the group, or perhaps just behind the group.

Teaching methods

Good, skilful teaching/coaching facilitates the learning of something worthwhile, and it is important that teachers/coaches should develop styles of working which are "personal" to them as individuals. Trying to copy somebody else's style is seldom, if ever, successful. Because teachers/coaches are frequently under pressure they sometimes develop a fixed approach to the task, and the pattern they establish might well be very similar to that established right back in the early days of their training courses. In order to broaden their background and appreciation of their role and task, teachers/coaches should seek opportunities:

- for watching others at work and discussing with them what they have seen
- to invite others to observe them at work, and then **listening** carefully to the comments arising from that experience
- to ask for comments from the class/group about the lesson and how it was received
- for attending seminars and courses designed to extend the skills of teaching/coaching, as well as knowledge of swimming.

Relationships

Teachers/coaches should recognise the wide range of relationships that their role embraces. Teacher/coach and pupil is probably the most obvious set of relationships, and the one this chapter has dealt with in some detail. However, others deserve to be noted so that teachers/coaches can give some thought to the issues which might arise:

- **pupil/pupil** – the interaction of the individuals within the group is a matter of some importance. Being alert for the cues mentioned earlier will assist in diffusing moments of tension, or perhaps influence groupings
- **teacher/coach and other teacher/coaches** – since a large proportion of the role of these people will be in close proximity to each other, the importance of maintaining a "professional" attitude and approach cannot be overstressed. Public arguments about how situations should or should not be handled, or the success or failure of particular drill or schedule do nothing to enhance the image of those concerned. Many topics are better debated privately or in a committee

● **teacher/coach and parents** – a great deal of the work of a teacher/coach is done with young people, and it is not, therefore, unusual for parents to be closely involved in what is happening. Occasionally they may have aspirations for their children which a qualified, experienced teacher/coach might feel are just not achievable. Unless this is dealt with in a professional and understanding manner then, at best, it could be very hurtful to the parent and, at worst, could result in some long term ill feeling and resentment which could pervade the general atmosphere of the future activities of a club or group.

Expecting parents to act simply as taxi drivers, and not express an interest in their children's progress is unreasonable and teachers/coaches should be prepared to make use of notes and records of achievement in their discussions with parents. Conversely, there are occasions where parents off-load their children without seeming to care about their progress. For the benefit and increased motivation of those children their teachers/coaches should try to find some way of helping those parents become more involved.

The role and task of the teacher/coach is not an easy one and cannot be simply stated as "Stand up, Speak up, Shut up!" Those with aspirations of becoming good, effective teachers/coaches should make every effort to consider the "professional" implications in their entirety. The learner at any level in the sport has the right to expect the best on offer. We should do our utmost to fulfil that expectation by providing the best.

Chapter 2

Acquisition of Skill

Dr Colin Lee

Introduction

This chapter is concerned with the factors which influence the learning of physical skills, with a particular reference to the early and intermediate stages of learning. It will be seen that effective teaching incorporates an understanding of the theoretical principles which govern how skill is learned and applies these principles to the structure of teaching sessions.

What is Skill?

Skill is a learned ability to reproduce specific patterns of movement which achieve desired outcomes. In swimming there is a general consensus about such outcomes in terms of the correct movement patterns of swimming strokes, dives, etc., and the teacher/coach is constantly comparing a learner's performance with an 'ideal model'. Skilful swimming has the characteristics of efficiency (using just as much effort as is needed) and permanence (can be repeated consistently).

Correct patterns of movement are usually referred to as techniques and a technique becomes a skill when it can to be adapted to meet changes in circumstances. This will be seen in accomplished swimmers who alter the arm action prior to a turn, or suddenly change direction in a crowded pool. In the early stages of learning the priority is to establish the solid foundation of good techniques upon which is built the progression towards becoming a skilful swimmer.

How is Skill Learned?

There will always be a small minority of people who appear to have a natural ability to swim – they have natural buoyancy, are completely at home in the water and appear to be able to swim as soon as they enter water for the first time. However, the majority of people have to learn the water confidence that comes so naturally to the fortunate few. The learning of skills is a progression through definite stages; individuals will start at different points, they will learn at different rates and they will have unique levels of potential. This final level of performance will be determined by a number of well-documented factors:

- physical, mental, social and emotional development
- natural ability
- availability of time and facilities
- quality of teaching/coaching.

The factor common to all individuals is the process that they go through in order to acquire a skill. This process is one of making a movement response to information received by the central nervous system. This information may come from external sources (extrinsic), e.g., that which is seen, heard or felt; alternatively, it may be from internal messages (intrinsic) about the position of limbs, balance, respiratory demands, etc. A learner's central nervous system has to handle all this information and then try to send messages to a variety of muscles in order to produce movement. Performance of a skill results from the successful processing of the relevant information and the selection of the correct muscular responses. The ways in which swimmers at different stages of learning are able to handle this information tell teachers/coaches much about the type of learning tasks which should be provided.

Non-Swimmers

The learner will focus on the external environment and the information that it provides, which is often counter-productive to the establishment and repetition of skilful movement. By attending to the feel of water (particularly on the face), to the movement of the water and to the presence of other people, the learner finds it difficult to simultaneously attend to the movement of limbs. The task of the teacher/coach is to bring learners to a state where they ignore much of this external information, i.e., they learn to ignore the effect of being in water. Play-like activities, buoyancy aids and, above all, frequent short periods in the water, all help to develop familiarisation with the effects of water. The effects become known, predictable and non-threatening. As a result, water becomes 'user-friendly' and the external information starts to require less conscious attention. Only when this level of water confidence is present can the learner really start to focus on developing the movement patterns of swimming.

Beginners

After plenty of opportunity to get used to being in water, the learner is observed to grow in confidence and start to feel at home in the water. If instruction in swimming strokes is presented while the learner's attention is still on external information, desired movement patterns are difficult to acquire. New movements require conscious thought and this, in turn, demands that the learner attends to the feel of movement. The beginner who is still worried about the effects of water will continue to concentrate on these effects and be unlikely to focus on performance of new movements; instead, the learner uses movements that do not have to be thought about, and resorts to the established pattern for locomotion on land – usually a combination of walking and crawling which we know as a 'Dog Paddle' or Front Paddle movement.

The progressive acquisition of swimming skills is dependent, to a great extent, on the learner being in a state where attention is concentrated on the internal messages resulting from movement, i.e., feedback. The learner must be able to store, in the memory, what a correct movement feels like and then recognise when the same feedback is experienced again. The task of the teacher/coach is to communicate to the learner that a movement is correct and to encourage the learner to remember what that movement feels like. This ability to store in the memory the feel of correct movements is an important stage in the progressive acquisition of skills. Good, experienced swimmers can also detect when the feedback is incorrect and can initiate corrections for themselves in order to return to the feedback that they know they should be experiencing.

Factors influencing Skill Learning

Having established the basic progression in information-handling at the heart of learning a skill, it is time to consider the aspects of learning and teaching that can help or hinder the subsequent essential progressions.

Motivation

The learner must **want** to learn and the teacher/coach must foster this desire. Young learners may get an intrinsic satisfaction from being able to move in the water, i.e., they may simply want to learn skills for their own sake. Alternatively, they may respond to extrinsic influences such as wanting to be like their friends or the desire to please the parent or teacher/coach who says that swimming is a good thing to learn. Rewards such as presents or awards, e.g., the ASA Awards Scheme, often strengthen the motivation. Adult learners may be driven by a mastery motive – a desire to overcome a sense of failure that was experienced earlier in life. It may be that the adult's wish to participate in a sport such as sailing or water-skiing can only be realised if the ability to swim is acquired.

In all these cases motivation will be maintained if the learner experiences frequent feelings of success because such feelings promote enjoyment and this, in turn, is the commonest motive for continued participation in any activity. The teacher's task is to ensure that activities are right for the individual learner's stage of development and that realistic goals are set for each individual. Every learner must leave every lesson with an overall feeling of satisfaction as a result of achieving the goals which were set.

Some learners will respond positively to competition although the individual's personality will determine, to a large extent, if competition is to be a motivating force. The role of the teacher/coach is to ensure that each individual benefits in some way from competition, thus the form of competition must be appropriate. Self-competition, where the learner attempts to improve on previous scores, times, etc, may well be more beneficial for some individuals than competition against others. The latter provides but one winner and teachers must be confident that losers are able to learn something from the experience of losing – an experience that can be de-motivating for young beginners. In the early stages of learning it will also be seen that competition almost inevitably leads to skill deterioration.

A positive aspect of competition is that it can provide a fun element in lessons as well as a challenge. Advanced swimmers will have to learn the 'skills' of competing – reaction time at starts, race strategies, etc. However, at every stage of learning teachers/coaches must give some thought to the organisation of swimmers. A swimmer should compete, in training, against someone of equal ability. It is far better to split a group into pairs of swimmers of equal ability, and have them compete against each other, than have a single race involving the whole group. The stage of learning, the type of competition, good organisation and sensitive teaching/coaching are the determinants of the true value of competition and its contribution towards the motivation of swimmers.

Visual Models

Vision is the dominant stimulus in the early stages of learning a skill. It can be a constraint, in the case of the non-swimmer who attends almost exclusively to what is seen, to the extent that all other responses may stop if vision is affected by the unfamiliar effect of water on the eyes. On the other hand, visual information can be a powerful teaching tool as learners progress towards mastery of the strokes.

Much physical learning occurs through imitation; this may be the result of casual observation of surrounding swimmers or by being directed to observe a particular response. The latter is obviously preferable because the quality of the model can be controlled and, as learners learn what they copy, the copying of incorrect responses must be avoided for the sake of future learning. Demonstrations enable learners to visualise the teaching/coaching points being made and they provide a model that is far easier to understand than that resulting from verbal instruction. Teaching/coaching methods that maximise this situation are the most beneficial for all learners. However, demonstrations lose their effectiveness if:

- learners are poorly positioned, e.g., the symmetry of Breaststroke cannot be seen from a side-on view; observers must be out of the water and in line with the demonstrator
- learners do not have an opportunity for practice immediately after a demonstration; they must get straight back in the water to try to reproduce the model
- air temperature is too low, thus making learners reluctant to leave the water and, when on poolside, distracted from the demonstration by their own coldness
- too much verbal instruction accompanies the demonstration; there must be just enough teacher/coach comment to inform learners of the one or two key teaching/coaching points to observe (this also reminds the demonstrator of the aspects of performance on which to concentrate).

Practice

Practice is very obviously a key factor in skill acquisition. There are two forms; mental rehearsal and physical practice.

Mental Rehearsal

This technique of visualising (imagining) the performance of a skill without actually doing it is a proven technique for helping to improve performance. As it requires the memory to send all the necessary messages for a particular movement to the appropriate muscles, only to stop short at actually producing the movement, it is necessary for a learner to have experienced the movement beforehand. Learners should be encouraged to imagine themselves performing the correct technique, recalling from memory those movements that they remember were correct because the teacher/coach told them at the time.

Physical Practice

Skill acquisition requires physical practice in a form that provides sufficient repetition of movements in order to produce an habital response. Once a movement is a habit it is no longer controlled by higher centres of the brain and there is no conscious effort to produce it, i.e., it does not have to be thought about. To achieve this aim it is necessary to consider both **what** is practised and **how** it is practised.

Learners learn what they practise and this dictates that, if the objective is skilful swimming, emphasis must be placed on good technique from the early stages. Bad habits are as easy to learn as good ones but, if incorrect responses become habitualised in the early stages, further improvements are often prevented, e.g., a 'screw kick' in the Breaststroke. The amount of repetition necessary for individuals to achieve permanence and consistency will vary from learner to learner. This requires teachers/coaches to plan programmes so that there is frequent revision of previous activities. This will give teachers/coaches opportunities to assess learners' retention and the learners themselves (especially young ones) will gain the satisfaction which arises from the performance of well-learned skills. New learning activities can prove frustrating for some individuals so they need opportunities to remind themselves of the skills that they can perform successfully. A good teaching/coaching session retains a balance of repetition of previous activities, development of previous activities and the introduction of two or three new experiences.

There are two potential constraints on the amount of repetition that a learner can tolerate. These are fatigue and boredom. The moment that a required movement pattern is breaking down, the practice must be stopped. If fatigue is the cause, the movement response becomes inefficient as the learner starts to use additional muscles in an effort to compensate for the muscles that are tired and, consequently, errors appear in the performance. Repetition of errors leads to habituation of errors, this must be avoided in all skill learning. Advanced swimmers are trained to develop an error detection mechanism which will produce reversion to correct movement as the onset of fatigue becomes apparent. However, such learning to maintain skill despite fatigue is beyond the capability of a beginner who is still in the process of establishing the skill. At this stage of learning, the activity must stop and a complete change introduced so that fatigued muscles are rested and the learner's interest is re-stimulated.

The early stages of acquiring swimming skills place considerable demands on the body's energy supply systems and physical fatigue is a frequent occurrence. In later stages of learning, the swimmer may suffer from mental, rather than physical, fatigue during long practice periods. These signs of lessening interest and enthusiasm should prompt teachers/coaches to change activities. Boredom is less of a problem for learners in the early and intermediate stages but its cause, should it arise, will be either that an activity is too difficult or that it is too easy. It is, therefore, essential that teachers/coaches are constantly monitoring the responses of individuals for changes in performance that might be resulting from fatigue or boredom. Teachers/coaches also have to consider the structure of practice sessions in terms of the length of sessions and the type of learning situations which meet the needs of individuals. The early stages of learning benefit from practice periods that are 'little and often'. The effects of fatigue and boredom have already been discussed and short, intense practices help to guard against such negative effects on learning. As skills are gradually acquired learners are able to maintain interest for longer periods and their efforts are applied more economically so that longer practice sessions are possible. The rest between practice sessions enables learners, if they are instructed to do so, to forget any incorrect responses in the last session and to practise mental rehearsal of the desired features of performance.

For many reasons a practice period should contain a variety of activity. This helps to maintain interest, relieves any localised muscle fatigue and has a long term effect of increasing skill learning. Variety of practice enables learners to become adaptable, to develop their own strategies for learning and to understand the subtle differences between the variety of skills that they are in the process of learning. The multi-stroke approach not only allows individuals to find a stroke that gives early success, but it also contributes towards the process of learning how to learn.

The most successful method of learning many skills has proved to be the approach known as Whole-Part-Whole and this is particularly appropriate for the acquisition of swimming skills. Learners are initially introduced to the whole skill, e.g., a stroke or a turn, etc. First attempts at the whole skill are observed by the teacher/coach who is looking for any parts of the skill that are weaker than others. The process of stroke analysis reveals such weaknesses. Learners are then provided with opportunity for specific practice of a part of the skill which appears to require attention. When the component part has improved, the whole stroke is immediately repeated and the teacher/coach looks for maintenance of the 'part-improvement' within the co-ordinated whole stroke. It may then be necessary for a different component to receive specific attention but it is always important for whole skills to be repeated after practice of any individual part.

Feedback

The most difficult task of the teacher/coach is to express the 'feel' of skill performance because efficient movement of the limbs relies on the learner recognising that the movement "feels right". This requires the learner to firstly know that a movement is correct and, secondly, to register how that movement felt.

"Feedback" is the term used for the mechanism that helps both these states to be achieved. Any action results in a feedback of information from muscles and joints about both the action itself and the results of the action. If, for example, a learner performs a complete Breaststroke and finds that forward momentum is achieved, the stroke is repeated and the subsequent momentum is compared with what was experienced the first time. If it feels different the learner wants to know why, and the source of the answer is the teacher/coach.

The role of the teacher/coach is three-fold. Firstly, learners must be informed when actions are correct, secondly, they must be instructed to concentrate on what the correct action felt like (so that they can recognise it again when it occurs) and, thirdly, the teacher/coach is the source of the corrective feedback, i.e., the changes that are necessary must be communicated. Usually, for best learning to occur, corrective feedback should be positive, i.e., what is wanted, rather than what is not wanted.

Teachers/coaches are, therefore, concerned with ensuring that learners attend to internal feedback and they are also the source of praise, which confirms correctness, and corrective information when errors occur. Praise is an important stimulus for learners. Whenever it is deserved, it must be provided. This can often be done non-verbally, by smiles and gestures, as the swimmer repeats the actions. The more immediate such feedback is, the more effective it is. Corrective feedback can also be communicated non-verbally in many cases, e.g., while the learner is still swimming, the teacher can face the swimmer and demonstrate arm action, pointing to elbow position or hand shape, etc.

Verbal communication by the teacher/coach will be pre-performance, during performance or post-performance. In the early stages of learning such instruction is best kept to a minimum when it is about the skill itself. One teaching/coaching point at a time is a good maxim for initial instruction. This also applies to comments after performance – these are very often concerned with guidance for correction of skills and learners cannot cope with a long list of errors to correct and performance factors to think about. During performance itself the beginner may fail to notice verbal instructions, although more accomplished swimmers will respond to a verbal cue provided they know beforehand that, for example, a shout of 'fingers' is a reminder to them to concentrate on that aspect of performance. Feedback can be seen to serve two vital objectives:

- the motivational function of praise
- the direction of learner attention to the internal information which is provided during task performance

Summary

The chapter has considered the acquisition of skills in terms of an information-processing model. The mechanisms and processes which are utilised for the initial learning, and then the gradual improvement of swimming skills, are all related to the way in which information is handled. The role of the teacher/coach is to control the amount and type of information to which learners must attend. This requires awareness of the needs and abilities of each individual swimmer and the presentation of experiences which provide the following essential pre-requisites for skill learning to occur:

- activities must be right for the individual
- learners must see a good model of any skill
- there must be ample opportunity for practice
- learners require knowledge of how they have performed
- every learner must experience the enjoyment that results from success

Chapter 3

Lesson plans, schedules and recording generally

Colin Hardy

Introduction

Pre-active teacher/coach behaviours, such as planning and evaluation, are the things a teacher/coach does to promote learning while no learners are present. They are the principal means by which the professional knowledge of the teacher/coach affects the process of teaching/coaching. For example, unless the teacher/coach is aware of the most appropriate learning activities for a particular group of non-swimmers, or of the type of training schedule that is best suited to a group of experienced swimmers preparing for a local championship, it is unlikely that the purpose of the lesson or schedule will be achieved.

Pre-planning

Before planning the lesson or training schedule the teacher/coach must have a knowledge of the group to be taught and of the resources available.

- **Knowledge of the group of students**
- experience of water
- experience of group swimming lessons
- general ability level
- ability range within the group
- size of the group

- **Knowledge of resources**
- water space available
- depth and temperature of the water
- poolside space available
- equipment available
- number of classes in the pool
- general acoustics of the pool

Once teachers/coaches have acquired such information they are then ready to plan their lessons or training schedules according to their own knowledge and skills. Knowledge would include an understanding of the fundamentals of the competitive strokes and the principles of training, and skills would include the ability to successfully communicate to a group.

Planning the lesson or training schedule

The objective of the lesson or training schedule should describe how swimmers are to perform after having had the swimming experience, and it should be stated at a level of specificity that makes it possible to recognize the behaviour should it be displayed. By making a clear statement of the intended outcome the objective provides criteria for the selection and presentation of content and cues for formulating evaluation procedures.

- **Objectives:** Examples – an objective can either predict behaviour expected at the end of the lesson or training schedule or provide swimmers with an invitation to explore or to focus on issues that are of interest to them.

- **Predictive objective:** Examples – swim a minimum of two widths Breaststroke showing a symmetrical leg action. Swim fifty metres Front Crawl in less than thirty-eight seconds.
- **Evocative objective:** Examples – find different ways of getting in and out of the hoops in shallow water. Find out the best consistent pace for each repetition of a set.

Some lessons and training schedules may need more than one objective and may include both predictive and evocative objectives.

- **Selection and presentation of content:** once the lesson or training schedule objectives have been established, the teacher/coach is in a position to make decisions on the selection and presentation of the content.
- **Selection of content:**

(a) Objective: swim a minimum of two widths Breaststroke showing a symmetrical leg action. Breaststroke kick teaching/coaching practices.

These could be carried out in both the prone and supine positions:
- holding the side
- gliding to the side
- towed by a partner
- holding a kick board
- holding a kick board for resistance
- with the arms either extended or behind the back
- using a gliding Breaststroke

Teaching/coaching points for swimmers to focus upon:
- bring the heels up to the seat
- cock and turn the feet outwards before the kick
- kick outwards, backwards and together
- sweep the legs round and together
- straighten the legs and the ankles during the kick

Questions for swimmers to answer:
- did you get your ankles to touch each other at the end of the kick?
- did you feel balanced during the recovery and the kick?
- did you feel that you were kicking with both legs equally?
- did you go straight forward after the kick?

(b) Objective: find out the best consistent pace for each repetition of a set.

Teaching/coaching practices:
- competitive strokes
- kicking
- pulling
- bi-lateral breathing
- single-arm swimming

Questions for swimmers to focus upon:
- did you maintain a consistency of pace at different distances?
- did you maintain a consistency of pace with different strokes?

>   – was it easier to maintain a consistent pace with part practices?
>   – does the breathing rhythm have any effect on the consistency of pacing?
>   – was it easier to maintain a consistent pace with some rest intervals than with others?

● **Presentation of content** Teacher:

     – verbal presentation using explanations, teaching/coaching points and questions
     – demonstrations by the teacher/coach or swimmer
     – use of visual aids (e.g., task cards)

Instructional organisation:
– class as whole
– group within class with pupils performing the same activity
– group within class with pupils performing the same activity but at different intensities
– group with pupils performing different activities individual tasks.

Pupil formations: See figures 3.1, 3.2 and 3.3

Figure 3.1 Pool use and pupil formations – example (a)

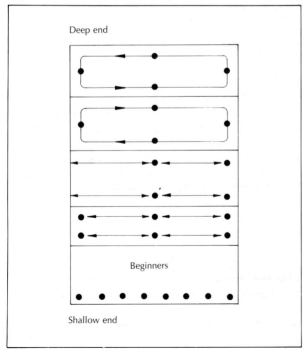

Figure 3.2 Pool use and pupil formations – example (b)

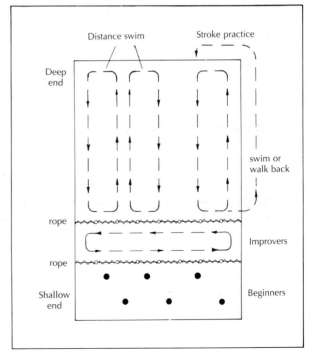

Figure 3.3 Pool use and pupil formations – example (c)

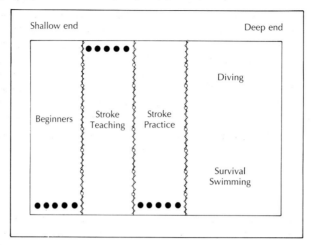

Evaluation procedures

Evaluation should be viewed as a continuous, ongoing, integral part of the learning process, and teachers/coaches will need to collect information on the swimmers' progress towards, and their accomplishment of, goals. Lessons/training schedules are evaluated in terms of the stated objectives, and the more specific the objectives the easier it is for teachers/coaches to evaluate outcomes. Information about swimmers is usually collected by teachers/coaches using informal methods, although the formal test at the end of a unit of work is sometimes used.

If the objective of the session is to "swim a minimum of two widths showing a symmetrical leg action" the teacher/coach may mentally note the pupils who are accomplishing the task or may design an observation-sheet to help in making the evaluation (Fig. 3.4).

Figure 3.4 Observation sheet

Tick box if the item is completed successfully		
	YES	NO
1. Swims two widths Breaststroke	[√]	[ ]
2. Demonstrates a symmetrical leg action	[ ]	[√]
3. If the answer to No. 2 is <u>NO</u>		
Is there a lack of symmetry at the: hips?	[ ]	[ ]
knees?	[√]	[ ]
feet?	[√]	[ ]

Sometimes teachers/coaches may wish to formalise the situation and carry out a series of tests at the end of a unit of work, for example, testing swimmers using the entry times for, say, county championships. In general teachers/coaches tend to use more informal methods of collecting data, e.g., anecdotal records, observation sheets, rating scales, as formal testing can be very time consuming. However, whatever the method used, the evaluation of performances should be guided by specific criteria based on clear objectives. Whilst many objectives used in swimming tend to be directed at the performance of swimmers, there may be occasions when teachers/coaches may be more concerned with other domains of learning. For example, promoting an understanding of streamlining in relation to stroke technique (cognitive domain), or encouraging the group to train as a team (social domain). In such cases the teacher/coach should still prepare objectives in a way that will provide cues for the evaluation procedures to take place.

Cognitive domain: explain to the teacher/coach how streamlining helps the speed of a stroke.

Social domain: co-operate as a group to ensure that the schedule is completed within forty minutes.

Hidden Messages

With all lessons/training schedules unplanned messages are communicated to pupils. The way in which teachers/coaches organize their lessons, e.g., assigning groups by ability or allowing pupils to decide upon their own groups, the kind of learning activities, e.g., co-operative or competitive practice situations and evaluation procedures, e.g., grading on understanding or performance, all pass silent messages on to the pupils. It is, therefore important for teachers and coaches to reflect upon their actions in case stated values are contradicted by their behaviour. For example, teachers/coaches who have planned for co-operative behaviours among their swimmers, but exhibit competitive behaviour themselves, may be communicating "mixed" messages.

Structure of the lesson or training schedule

Although the prime purpose of the lesson/training schedule is to fulfil the objectives, such concepts as **balance, pace** and **variety** are important if pupil interest is to be maintained:

Balance: Are the pupils spending too much time on one practice?
            Is there too much leg work in the schedule?

Pace: Are the pupils spending too much time listening?
         Are the pupils waiting too long between sets of repetitions?

Variety: Are there different ways of practising a movement?
            Should all lessons/training schedules include some contrasting activity, i.e., a subsidiary objective?

Each session should be seen by pupils as one of a series of lessons/schedules, and they should be able to relate fundamental information to different aquatic activities. For example, the most common type of lesson plan or training schedule tends to involve five phases, viz: introductory activity, main theme, contrasting activity, concluding activity and supervised free activity. However, phases may be added or subtracted depending upon the prepared objectives.

Lesson plan

Phase

1 **Introductory activity:** Teachers/coaches should *either* relate the activity to work performed in a previous lesson *or* just select a known activity that will quickly involve the swimmers.

2 **Main theme:** Teachers/coaches should:
- relate the activities to the main objective
- give a brief explanation of the work
- give a demonstration of the skill if appropriate
- organise as appropriate for class or group instruction
- be prepared to modify objectives if necessary

3 **Contrasting activity:** Teachers/coaches should *either* relate the activity to an on going subsidiary theme *or* select a contrasting activity that reinforces previous work or prepares for future activities.

4 **Concluding activity:** Teachers/coaches should:
- reinforce the points crucial to fulfilling the objectives
- check whether objectives have been fulfilled
- give the swimmers an assessment of their performances, and indicate how the work will be developed.

5 **Supervised free practice:** Teachers/coaches should ensure that these activities are safe.

Teacher/coach function during activity

Interactive teacher/coach behaviours are those behaviours which occur in the presence of pupils. They are the means by which a teacher/coach affects pupil learning activities, and through them, learning outcomes:

- **a safe learning environment** – experienced teachers/coaches learn to anticipate safety problems and build safety into the tasks they give and arrange space and pupils so that learning takes place in a safe environment. However, teachers/coaches must always be prepared to interfere if conditions are unsafe as this must take precedence over all other concerns. In some cases it may be necessary to change the activity and in other situations it may be enough to restrict the activity to certain individuals in a specific part of the pool.

- **clarity of instruction** – teachers/coaches should be prepared to think through the language they intend using in the presence of the class. Confusion can sometimes result if teachers/coaches:
  - do not state the task clearly
  - use too technical language
  - talk when pupils' faces and ears are underwater
  - do not take into account the acoustics of the pool

If the pupils are not responding in the desired way the teacher/coach should be prepared to stop a class, a group or an individual and repeat the task to reinforce on-task behaviour.

- **Maintaining on-task behaviour** – there are times during a lesson/training schedule when pupils do not respond in the desired way, even though the task instructions have been clearly delivered. In such circumstances teachers need to look for causes of such off-task behaviours and respond accordingly.

For example, weak swimmers may be losing interest because they are being over-challenged by the activity, or experienced swimmers may start to misbehave because they are bored by the repetitive practices. In such cases teachers/coaches may find it necessary to adjust the content of the lesson/ training schedule (see also task appropriateness).

● **Feedback** – feedback is a means of providing pupils with information about their performances, and tends to serve as a motivating function. Feedback can be either evaluative or corrective and can be used in a negative or positive form to a class, a group or an individual (Fig 3.5). Evaluative feedback occurs when a value judgement is made about a pupil's performances and then directly communicated to that pupil. Corrective feedback provides the pupil with advice on what to do or on what not to do. In using feedback teachers/coaches must take into consideration the pupils and their level of ability. For example, corrective positive feedback may be more helpful with pupils who are making consistent errors, general positive feedback may motivate pupils who are making many different errors and general negative feedback may have the desired effect on those who are making little effort. As a general rule, where possible, use corrective **positive** feedback as soon as possible after a performance.

Figure 3.5 Examples of types of feedback used in swimming

	Feedback	
	Evaluative	**Corrective**
General	"a good swim"	"put more effort into it"
Specific	"you got the elbows nice and high in that swim"	"pull with the elbow up"
Negative	"you didn't hold the time for the last repetition"	"don't bend your legs"
Positive	"you are holding your pace well"	"pull closer to the centre line"
Class	"you have all made improvements during the lesson"	"you must all remember to breathe out under water"
Group	"the swimmers in lane one have not worked hard enough this session"	"remember to start five seconds behind the swimmer in front"
Individual	"you haven't got the timing right"	"kick down at the beginning of the arm pull"

N.B. Categories are not mutually exclusive.

Task appropriateness

At times teachers/coaches may find that the work they have planned needs modifying. Swimmers may have to be given longer rests between practices; some may have to be changed to less competitive groups, whilst others may have to be given different tasks. It is unlikely that any plan will cater for all individuals and, therefore, teachers/coaches must be prepared to make the necessary adjustments when the need arises.

Sample Lesson Plan

Date: 1/9/90

Class:
Age: 8 years
Ability: Non-swimmers and beginners
Number: 10

Length of lesson: 30 minutes

Depth of water: 0.8 to 1.0 metres

Objectives:
1. Demonstrate alternating and simultaneous arm and leg movements supported by arm bands.
2. Demonstrate either an alternating or simultaneous type of swimming stroke (with or without arm bands).
3. Play a ball game showing the ability to move in the water with the feet off the bottom of the pool (with or without arm bands).

Equipment:
10 pairs of arm bands
10 kickboards
5 balls

Phase	Practice	Communication of task	Instructional cue/question	Organisation	Reason for practice
1. Introductory activity (3 mins)	Enter the water and walk behind partner	Explanation	"Slide the feet along the bottom of the pool"	Pairs organised prior to the pupils entering the water; arm bands placed on pupils prior to entering the water; pupils work within roped off area; pupils change the leader at a signal	Relate to activity in previous lesson
2. Main theme (i) (13 mins)	Hold a float: kick legs with alternating movements	Teacher/coach demonstrates an alternating movement using the arms with explanation	Can you kick when you are on your front, on your back and on your side?	Place kickboards along the side of the pool to be collected by the pupils; all pupils to keep arm bands on	Objective 1

32

	(ii)	Hold a float: kick legs with simultaneous movement	Teacher/coach demonstrates a simultaneous movement using the arms with explanation	Can you copy your partner's movement?		Objective 1
	(iii)	Pull with alternating arm movements	Teacher/coach demonstrates an alternating movement with explanation	Can you move your arms, over and under the water?	Place kickboard on the side but keep arm bands on	Objective 1
	(iv)	Pull with simultaneous arm movements	Teacher/coach demonstrates a simultaneous movement with explanation	Can you pull when you are on your back and front? Can you copy your partner's movement?		Objective 1
	(v)	Co-ordinate **either** alternating arm and leg movements **or** simultaneous arm and leg movements	Teacher/coach demonstrates different kinds of strokes and gives names to the strokes	Show me a proper stroke now. Did you move forwards with the stroke?	Arm bands to be taken off or retained at the discretion of pupils; pupils who take off their arm bands to be monitored closely	Objective 2
3. Contrasting activity (6 mins)		Play a ball game with partner	Explanation	Can you kick yourself upwards before throwing? Can you use your left and your right hand? Can you use both hands at once? Can you throw the ball close to your partner? Can you catch the ball?	Arm bands at the discretion of pupils; check that pupils are not far from partners	Objective 3

4. Concluding activity (4 mins)	Practise arm and leg movements of a recognised stroke	Explanation	Do you know the name of the stroke you are trying?	Arm bands at the discretion of the pupils	Objective 2
5. Supervised free practice (4 mins)		Explanation		Check for any unsafe practices	Opportunity for pupils to make responsible decisions

General notes: Maintain a "buddy" system.
Check own positioning and voice for effectiveness.
Give appropriate feedback to as many pupils as possible.
Maintain pace between activities.
Be prepared to modify or change the content of the lesson or the time planned for each phase.

	YES	NO
Evaluation procedures: Did the majority of the pupils achieve the three objectives?	[ ]	[ ]
Did you monitor all pupils?	[ ]	[ ]
Do any pupils need special attention?	[ ]	[ ]
Have you made a record of individual performances?	[ ]	[ ]

Sample Schedule

Date: 1/9/90

Group: Age: 12 years
       Ability: Average club swimmers
       Number: 20

Length of schedule: 40 minutes

Length of pool: 25 metres

Objectives: 1. Carry out the schedule keeping to the exact rest periods
       2. Show the ability to maintain a consistent pace on each repetition of a set
       3. Recover the arms in Front Crawl using a high elbow technique.

Equipment: 20 pull buoys
       20 kickboards
       Large sweep clock

Phase	Practice	Communication of task	Instructional cue/question	Organisation	Reason for practice
1. Introductory activity (6 mins)	250 to 300 metres of Front Crawl **Lanes one and two:** swim 300 metres **Lanes three and four:** swim 250 metres. (4mins approximately) 2 mins rest (teacher/coach controls time)	Explanation	Can you recover with the elbow high?	Four lanes: **lanes one and three** swim clockwise, **lanes two and four** anti-clockwise; swimmers go off at 5 second intervals	Introduction to objective 3
2. Main theme (i) (12 mins)	Full stroke, Front Crawl **Lanes one and two:** 8×25 **on** 30 secs 4×50 **on** 60 secs 2×100 **on** 2 mins (12 mins) **Lane three and four:** 8×25 **on** 35 secs 4×50 **on** 1 min 10 secs *20 secs rest* 1×100 **on** 2 min 20 secs (12 mins) *2 mins rest* (teacher/coach controls time)	Explanation	Can you keep to the "off" times?	Fastest swimmer goes first in each lane and the slowest swimmer last; short-sighted swimmers will need help from others in keeping to the times; leading swimmer in each lane controls time between sets; place schedules on white/black boards	Objective 1
(ii)	**Lanes one and two:** 6×75 pull **on**	Explanation	Were your repetitions in each set at a	Pull buoys and kickboards assembled at	Objective 2

(17 mins)	1 min 40 secs *20 secs rest* 4×50 kick **on** 1 min 10 secs *20 secs rest* 4×25 full stroke **on** 25 secs (17 mins) **Lanes three and four:** 5×75 pull **on** 1 min 55 secs *20 secs rest* 4×50 kick **on** 1 min 20 secs *15 secs rest* 3×25 full stroke **on** 30 secs (17 mins)		consistent pace? Did you continually check the speed of yours swims?	end of each lane	
3. Contrasting practice (3 mins)	150 to 200 metres Front Crawl **Lanes one: and two:** swim 200 metres **Lanes three and four:** swim 150 metres (3 mins approximately) Move immediately into phase 4	Demonstration with explanation	"Keep the elbow high" "Lift with the elbow and reach with the hand"	Coach to be prepared to stop swimmers to give appropriate feedback	Objective 3
4. Concluding activity	Full stroke, Back Crawl. Swim for 2 mins	Explanation	Can you maintain a consistent pace?	Swimmers to adjust order in lane according to Back Crawl ability	Objective 2

General notes: Be prepared to adjust **D**istance, **I**nterval, **R**est and **T**ime (DIRT).
                        Be prepared to change swimmers' positions in a lane.
                        Be prepared to change swimmers from one lane to another.
                        Be prepared to modify or change the content of the schedule if the need arises.
                        Ensure that assistants understand your objectives.
                        Give appropriate feedback to as many pupils as possible.

                                                                                        YES NO
Evaluation procedures: Did the majority of the swimmers achieve the objectives?   [ ] [ ]
                        Did you (and your assistants) monitor all swimmers?   [ ] [ ]
                        Are you satisfied with the number of groups?   [ ] [ ]
                        Have you made a record of students' performances?   [ ] [ ]

Chapter 4

Equipment

Tony Holmyard

Introduction

Pick up any catalogue of swimming goods and you will appreciate the large selection of equipment available to help those engaged in learning, teaching, coaching or managing swimming activities.

The range of equipment

Equipment may be designed to give confidence to nervous beginners, help in the learning and development of skills and to increase enjoyment by adding to the variety of activities that can be attempted. Competitive swimmers use aids to improve their flexibility, muscular endurance and further develop their skills. Pool managers provide equipment to ensure the safety of pool users, to organise the best use of water space and time to enable competitors in the different swimming disciplines to be able to participate effectively. There is a vast array of buoyancy aids, sinking objects, floating objects, paddles, fins, goggles, hoops, clocks, ropes, safety equipment, etc. Since budgets are nearly always limited, well-informed selection is essential. This chapter is not designed to give definitive answers or to recommend 'Best Buys', but to point out some of the advantages and disadvantages of equipment so that those involved may make the most appropriate choices according to their circumstances, the needs of pupils and the resources available. When requesting or purchasing equipment bear in mind some of these considerations:

● is the equipment safe to the user or those close by?
● does it contribute significantly to learning, to further development of skill, to safety standards, or enjoyment?
● is it durable and with few maintenance problems?
● can it be stored securely in available space and be made readily available when required?
● is it suitable for general use, or is it limited to a few special individuals or circumstances?
● can the financial outlay be justified?

Swimming aids for non-swimmers normally consist of some form of buoyancy aid that can be securely attached to the body so that the non-swimmer will float with feet clear of the pool bottom and the head safely above water level, enabling the wearer to practise simple stroke techniques with some confidence. To increase the likelihood of learning to swim practices need to be enjoyable, varied and offer little chance of failure. Clearly, well designed buoyancy aids do much to improve these conditions. If the beginner has confidence that he will remain afloat, he is much more likely to take his feet off the bottom, let go of the poolside and travel across the pool using dynamic and enjoyable practices which are directly related to the skill of swimming.

Some teachers/coaches claim that pupils can become over-reliant on buoyancy aids and are reluctant to take them off. This tendency can be offset by making it clear from the outset that the additional support is only an initial phase of learning and that, once the basic movements are understood, the extra buoyancy should be reduced or removed soon after. Learners, themselves, are sometimes sensitive to the fact that buoyancy aids identify them as non-swimmers and some may be eager to dispense with them prematurely. Good teachers/coaches will be aware of this and may need to encourage the learner to retain the extra support until the right moment. Swimming aids that can have the degree of buoyancy progressively reduced are obviously preferable. The exact degree of buoyancy is not very critical, but the nervous beginner may need a little reassurance from the teacher/coach that it is sufficient to keep him afloat. Others may need reassurance that their 'public image' is not at risk by using buoyancy aids and that it is a perfectly normal stage for learners. Buoyancy aids, by their very nature, make it difficult, if not impossible, to practise submersion skills. Either the aid needs to be removed, or the skill postponed.

Inflatable rings

These were commonly used in the past, but they have some disadvantages. Adventurous youngsters often dive or plunge forward vigorously and the ring can slip down below the centre of gravity then continue to support the body, but in the inverted position. Confident beginners will often jump in and risk slipping through the ring and finding themselves out of their depth. If used, rings should be close-fitting and incorporate a diagonal shoulder strap to prevent movement down the body.

Arm bands

These are a better proposition, especially if each arm-band has two air chambers and each chamber has both an internal safety valve and a separate sealing plug. It is important that the correct size is used for each person so as to avoid little children using very large arm-bands which impede their movements, may contain too much buoyancy or may be less securely attached. Correct size selection also avoids larger people attempting to squeeze into arm-bands that are too small, which may not only reduce the blood supply to the arms, but also fail to provide sufficient support. The best type have a flat, non-inflatable area which is designed to fit against the inside of the arm and causes less interference with arm movements.

Beginners need to understand that arm-bands only afford support when immersed, so pupils should be taught practices that keep the arms in the water. It is time consuming for the teacher/coach alone to fit arm-bands to a large group, so pupils need to be shown how to assist each other by holding them open for the wearer to push the arm in till the aid is secure above the elbow, with the teacher/coach simply checking. They need not be deflated at the end of each lesson with the necessity of later reinflation. The arm-band can be stored in a plastic sack or threaded on to a length of cord for carrying or storage. Arm-bands are safe, cheap and not adversely affected by chlorinated water. Their level of buoyancy can be gradually reduced as pupils gain in confidence. Similar devices are available in the form of polystyrene discs with arm-holes off-centre. One or more discs can be slid onto the arm according to the level of support required. They are less robust than inflatable arm-bands but do a similar job and are quite effective.

Other learning aids

These appear on the market from time to time, e.g., 'Bubble Vests'. Other aquatic sports use 'Buoyancy Aids' or full life-jackets as an essential safety precaution, but these are normally too cumbersome for swimming practices and are also very expensive.

The 'Polyotter Suit' (originally the 'Stubton Suit') has its devotees. It consists of a full-size stretch swim suit with built in pouches just above the waist which contain cylinders of polystyrene. The pouch openings face downwards and buoyancy can be progressively reduced by slipping the cylinders out as swimmers gain in confidence. A variety of sizes is needed to give well-fitting suits to individuals and it does take a little time to sort out the correct size and to get the pupils into them with the appropriate amount of buoyancy for each one. Keeping the suits in good conditions also takes a little time. They should be rinsed in fresh water to prevent them deteriorating due to chemicals in pool water. They need to be hung up to dry after use. These suits are expensive. However, they do give great confidence and buoyancy can easily be regulated. One might hesitate to purchase large quantities for use with large groups because a proportion of beginners are usually confident enough to strike out without much assistance, but certainly the suits would be helpful with very anxious individuals or for early stages with small groups. All buoyancy aids should be selected with great care.

Figure 4.1 "Polyotter" suit.

Figure 4.2 Arm bands.

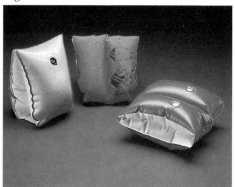

Figure 4.3 Polystyrene discs.

Hoops

Most hoops on the market today are made of plastic and may float, or may have a small weight incorporated into the construction so that they sink. The floating variety may be tethered at a chosen depth by attaching a weight or plastic container filled with gravel by a cord of appropriate length. The hoops are usually about one metre in diameter and are used to practise surface diving and underwater swimming.

40

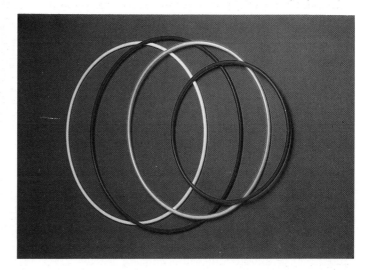

Left: Figure 4.4(a) Weighted hoop.

Figure 4.4(b) Variety of hoops.

Sinking objects

Items such as rubber-covered bricks are also used to encourage swimmers to surface dive, to open the eyes with confidence and to practise the search and retrieval skills of life saving. Small brightly coloured plastic sticks, or rings of about 15 centimetres diameter are used for the same purpose. They, too, are often weighted so that they sink to the bottom to stand vertically.

Figure 4.5(a) Sinking objects – selection (a).

Figure 4.5(b) Sinking objects – selection (b).

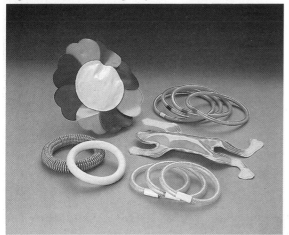

Large inflatable tubes

These can provide endless fun for youngsters to ride on, tow, race in, etc., but they are potential hazards and need constant supervision. Some are purpose-built with streamlined inflation valves, but inner tubes from cars or lorries need to have the protruding valves taped down to avoid minor injuries. Children often become excited using the rings, jostle and push each other, or tip the rings over. Teachers/coaches need to watch carefully for swimmers surfacing beneath the rings and to ensure that no boisterous activity goes on too near the edge of the pool where a falling pupil could strike the hard edge.

Figure 4.6 Large inflatable tube.

Kicking-board or floats

Floats are short boards of buoyant material, commonly polystyrene or closed-cell polyethylene foam, which come in several sizes from 30-45 centimetres in length and 22-30 centimetres in width and are usually 2.5-5 centimetres thick. The cheaper polystyrene variety tend to crumble easily and young children are tempted to pick at them or even chew pieces out of them, which is not only bad for their digestion, but carries a small risk of pieces sticking in the throat and obstructing breathing. They also tend to compress when stood upon. The more expensive models are more resilient and last much longer. A less common form of float is the 'Barbell' type which consists of a pole with a float at each end. It offers similar support but is more easily grasped by beginners. They take up more space in the water which might be a point to consider if working

Figure 4.7 Kicking boards and floats.

with large groups, and are less convenient to store. The kicking-board is easier to store. Both are unaffected by chlorinated water. Floats are normally held in the hands in order to provide support and to concentrate attention on the leg action of a stroke, either for skill development or for physical conditioning of the legs. As they are not attached to the body, they are less safe for beginners and must be used under close surveillance, preferably in a shallow water area or by pupils wearing other buoyancy aids. Kicking-boards are commonly used by those who can already swim, so that leg actions can be perfected in a variety of ways either prone or supine. Experienced swimmers also use them for support to isolate the legs in order to exercise the arms. This is done by trapping the float between the thighs. The size of float needs to be appropriate to the size of the swimmer so that he floats in a normal position, then the arm action may be practised realistically.

Figure 4.8 Pull-buoys.

Pull-buoys

A more specialised piece of equipment for arm action practices is the pull-buoy, which may be a solid one piece block of buoyant material shaped to fit between the thighs, or made up to two short cylinders loosely linked by cords so that the legs can be closed between them leaving one cylinder at the front and the other at the back of the thighs. Both types are popular with more experienced swimmers. They are easily stored and require little or no maintenance.

Hand paddles

These are pieces of flat plastic, a little larger than the area of the hand, which are worn on the palm of the hand and kept in place by finger loops. Competitive swimmers use them to create added resistance to the arm action in order to improve muscular strength and endurance. They are controversial in that they alter arm action resistance and, therefore, require adjustments to the technique of the unaided action. Some claim that they contribute to muscle soreness in the elbow and shoulder regions. They also pose a small risk to fellow swimmers when training under crowded conditions, in that the tough plastic edge can inflict scrapes to others close by if the arms are recovered carelessly. It may be wise to restrict their use to occasions when space and numbers allow and to avoid prolonged practice.

Figure 4.9 Hand paddles.

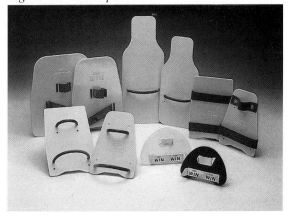

Figure 4.10 Fins.

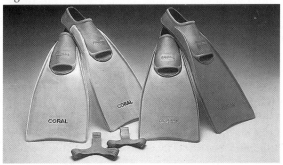

Fins

These are occasionally used by beginners to increase propulsion from the legs in crawl-type strokes, but fins are difficult to walk in, either on land or in the water, and may cause cramp in muscles unaccustomed to such vigorous work. More frequently they are used by competitive swimmers in training to improve ankle flexibility or simply to add fun to a training routine by increasing swimming speed. It is difficult to hold the range of sizes required by individuals without purchasing large numbers of fins. Swimmers also need to be aware of the danger to others, especially if surface diving, as they can deliver a nasty slap in the face to anyone close behind. Inexperienced swimmers need to be alerted to the danger of colliding with the pool wall as they will undoubtedly be travelling faster than normal when using fins.

Anti-chlorine goggles

If water in swimming pools is kept in good condition goggles should not be necessary for people swimming for short periods. Beginners do waste an awful lot of time trying to cope with goggles in order to keep the water away from their eyes. Many teachers/coaches regard it as essential early experience to deal with splashes to the face and to be able to open the eyes under water with confidence, and wearing goggles precludes this. However, people training for prolonged periods for general fitness purposes or in preparation for competitions probably do need them. Goggles do protect sensitive eyes from the irritation of pool chemicals and they give clear underwater vision which helps to avoid collisions in crowded lanes. Competitors find them useful in practicing racing turns where a clear view of the wall is important when approaching the end of a lap at speed. They also assist swimmers to refine their arm actions as the limb tracks can be more accurately observed during training. To be effective, goggles must fit the boney facial structure of the individual and also be tightly fitted. There is a good range of shapes and sizes on the market and care should be taken to find a good fit. The better ones incorporate an anti-fog film on the lens and are less prone to misting over. It helps if greasy fingers are kept off the lenses but, when they do mist over, a little saliva can be applied with the tongue or finger-tips to keep them clear. Unless beginners are particularly sensitive to pool chemicals they should try to manage without goggles until they have developed the confidence to cope with water

Figure 4.11 Anti-chlorine goggles.

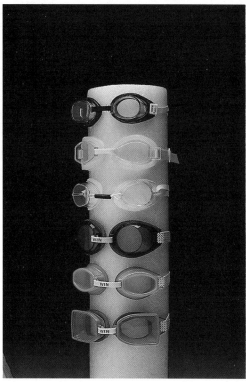

in contact with the face. In the early stages they could spend a great deal of time tipping water out of the goggles and adjusting their position instead of paying attention to the teacher/coach. All users of goggles should be taught to put them on and take them off safely by sliding them down or up the forehead. If pulled forward away from the face, they can easily slip from wet fingers and deliver a dangerous blow to the eye balls as the elastic recoils.

Items of equipment for teachers and coaches

Whistle

Whether metal or plastic a whistle should have a sharp, penetrating note which will readily attract the attention of pupils during noisy conditions or in an emergency. It should be reserved for such situations and not used to indicate other procedures such as starting an activity. The whistle's power to attract attention or stop all activity should not be diminished or confused by a variety of uses.

44

Figure 4.12 Clip-boards

Clip-boards

A clip-board is a useful memory aid, especially if sessions have a complex content, or a series of different activities follow on in succession. Lesson plans and training schedules can be referred to quickly and it is also handy for noting down ideas, individual corrections or achievements as they occur, which leads to better planned future sessions. Notes can be transferred later to a record book. A clip-board should be covered with waterproof material on the outside and contain a clear plastic sheet to protect the inner writing section from inevitable splashes.

Recording book

This is probably most useful in the form of a loose-leaf file. Lessons or training plans can be stored for reference which helps to promote orderly progression within any scheme of work. Teachers and coaches not only need to record the progress made by pupils for future report writing, but they need a convenient system for self-assessment so that their own performance is being constantly reviewed and upgraded.

Pole

In addition to the long rescue poles which are part of every pool's safety equipment, teachers/coaches may find a shorter light-weight pole, such as a broom handle of about 2 metres in length, to be a useful item when working with non-swimmers and beginners. It can be used to assist someone straying out of their depth but, more often, it will be used as a 'confidence-booster' when held within easy reach of an inexperienced swimmer who is attempting something new, such as swimming without buoyancy aids or going into deep water for the first time. The pole may have a short cross-bar or a loop of hose-pipe securely attached to the end to provide a more easily grasped handhold, but it does need to be **securely** attached. Provided the other members of the group are under safe supervision, the teacher/coach may walk along the side of the pool with the pole just preceding a swimmer attempting a prone stroke or just above the chest of one swimming on the back, so that they know assistance is immediately at hand. As confidence grows it may be held further away by mutual consent.

Pool equipment

As a general rule the provision of pool equipment is the responsibility of the Pool Manager, but teachers and coaches should be aware of what is required to teach or coach effectively and to organise competitions when required. They should also be prepared to report damage or deterioration of equipment so that high standards of provision can be maintained.

Safety equipment

All pools should contain a variety of rescue apparatus spaced around the pool in easily accessible sites. This includes long, light poles for reaching rescues and lifebuoys or torpedo buoys for throwing rescues, so that those responsible for safety can select the most appropriate aid to match the circumstances. A good first-aid kit should always be ready for use. Opinions vary about the desirability for breathing apparatus.

If it is available, it must be regularly maintained and checked and personnel must be thoroughly familiar with its function and be regularly re-trained in its use. An alternative view is that it is simpler and more effective to have staff qualified in, and regularly retrained in, Expired Air Resuscitation (E.A.R.).

Lane lines

Lane lines are essential pieces of equipment for well-managed pools. They are ropes of the correct length to divide the pool into graded lanes so that lap swimming, competitive training or competitions can be easily organised. Shorter lengths of rope should be available to divide off areas across the width so that different activities can be conducted simultaneously without interference with each other. The lines should incorporate floats every 60-100 centimetres. For competition 'anti-wave' lane ropes are desirable. These consist of buoyant discs which spin and absorb wave energy and so keep the water surface relatively calm. They are much more expensive and are bulky to store.

Right: Figure 4.13(a) "Anti-wave" lanes.
Below: Figure 4.13(b) Rope lane with floats.

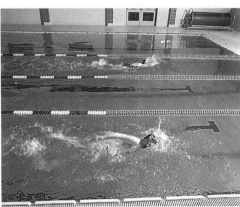

Figure 4.14 Mobile notice.

Mobile notices

These can be in the form of cones or plastic boards carrying simple information, such as the direction of rotation within each lane and the lane speed grade, e.g., fast, medium, slow. This helps lap swimming to be conducted with minimal supervision, little conflict and a low risk of collisions.

Blackboards

It is useful to have at least one mobile board which can be sited at a strategic point so that people entering the pool can be informed of any special conditions or arrangements for that session. Other boards may be permanently fixed to walls at convenient points where there is space for swimmers to gather and refer to work schedules, technical explanations or tactics, e.g., water-polo. Boards tend to deteriorate rapidly in damp atmospheres and need regular maintenance.

Pace clock

These come in a variety of sizes, the large ones being about one metre in diameter which enables them to be seen by most people from anywhere in the pool, especially if they are mounted above head height. Some are portable and can be placed near the end of the pool enabling swimmers to time their own activities. They are used to control teaching and coaching sessions for individuals and groups. If a clock runs off mains electricity it must be mounted well out of the reach of swimmers. Battery models can be used in 'wet areas', of course.

Figure 4.15 Pace clocks.

Starting blocks

Starting blocks should conform to ASA specifications. They should be easily fixed to the starting point so that they are absolutely secure and do not rock. Good blocks will offer a choice of hand holds for Backstrokers and a leading top edge that can readily be grasped by swimmers using a 'grab start'. To reduce the risk of swimmers hitting the bottom of the pool starting blocks should not be used in very shallow water. The minimum depth of water recommended **for experienced and properly prepared swimmers** is 0.9 metres, but constant reference should be made to current ASA guidelines on this important safety topic.

Backstroke warning flags

Wherever possible flagged ropes should be stretched across the pool 1.8 metres above the water surface from fixed supports or stands set at five metres from each end of the pool. They serve to warn Backstrokers that they are approaching the wall so that novices are less likely to hit the wall with their head and competitive swimmers quickly learn the number of strokes to the turn or finish from the moment they pass under the flags.

False start rope

During competitions a rope should be provided to stop swimmers in the event of a false start. Ideally, it is suspended across the pool from fixed stands fifteen metres in front of the starting end and may be dropped onto the water surface by a quick release mechanism. If stands are not available it can be hand-held.

Water polo equipment

Goals, a ball, caps and flags are needed to stage a game of water polo, but these items are also useful for teachers/coaches organising a variety of other aquatic games.

Notice boards

Apart from displaying regulations and instructions at different sites within a pool, e.g., foyer, changing rooms, poolside, noticeboards can provide attractive visual images and explanations which may be valuable to anyone learning particular techniques.

Figure 4.16 Storage containers.

Equipment storage

Shelves, mobile containers and cages help to keep items of equipment in good condition, keep the poolside clear of obstructions, enhance the appearance of the pool generally and can offer greater security for many small items.

Acknowledgement

The photographs in this chapter have been reproduced by kind permission of the Directors of "Swim Shop", 52-58 Albert Road, Luton LU1 3PR.

PART II

EXERCISE, HEALTH AND SAFETY

Introduction to Part II

The importance of a healthy lifestyle has been much emphasised by the medical profession and various health education groups during the last few years. Healthy lifestyle programmes have as their focal points the topics of exercise and nutrition. Clearly, the former needs the latter if it is to be maintained as a useful and sensible contribution to the individuals concerned. This is true at all levels of participation from the "Mr/Mrs Average in the street", who just want to lose a little weight or "keep in trim", to the competitor in training whose workload is far beyond that level. There is now a far greater understanding and emphasis on the need not only to eat enough, but also to eat enough of the right things. A considerable amount of research has been carried out in this sphere and Part II is designed to help the reader link the elements of exercise and nutrition so that eventually their performers will benefit from the advances in knowledge. Unfortunately, issues of nutrition and sporting performance are often blurred by the pressures and hype of the business world.

Concerns for safety should never take anything but the first priority for any teacher/coach. References to this topic in Part II are again designed to raise levels of awareness and provide some definite starting points for those who are new to the role of teacher/coach.

Chapter 5

Health, Safety and Hygiene
Alan Donlan

Introduction
Whilst it is assumed that the teacher/coach is in the business of fitness, it must be remembered that fitness is part of a wider concept of the healthy lifestyle. Concientious teachers/coaches should have an awareness of this and be setting standards for those in their charge to follow.

Health
It is now firmly established that anyone wanting a healthy lifestyle should take part in some form of regular physical activity. The type and level of this activity must take account of the age, general fitness and medical condition of the individual. One form of exercise which might be appropriate to one person in an age-group may be quite inappropriate for another of the same age. Not least among the benefits of swimming is the development and maintenance of good health for everyone, regardless of age, type and physical condition, including those with some disability. These benefits include:

- improvements in the condition of the heart and cardiovascular system in general
- increased physical capacity
- improvement in the control of an individual's body composition by helping to burn up some of the fat stores
- contribution to helping to control stress
- the promotion of a feeling of physical well-being
- a long term reduction in the risk of developing coronary heart disease

The advantages of swimming arise from the following two factors:

- the body is supported by the upthrust of the water
- the push and pull forces created by the muscles are directed against water rather than a solid medium, such as a road surface, thereby reducing the risks of injury, especially to ligaments and joints.

Regular exercise benefits the strength, stamina and suppleness of the body (often known as "the 3Ss").

Strength
Muscles which are not used tend to deteriorate and waste away, i.e., "use it or lose it" theory. Regular exercise reduces the likelihood of this happening and maintains or improves the size, strength and efficiency of muscles and muscle groups.

Stamina
People who take little or no exercise usually become breathless quickly when involved in any sudden exertion; they experience a rapid pulse rate which takes a considerable time to recover to its norm and

they tire easily, requiring frequent rests. Regular exercise increases the efficiency of the heart, blood circulation and breathing which lead to improved stamina. A further effect of this improved efficiency is the reduction in the risk of heart disease.

Suppleness

Joints which do not experience their full range of movement regularly tend to stiffen – a condition which normally becomes worse with age and may lead to greatly reduced mobility and problems with posture. Regular exercise considerably delays the onset of these conditions.

Sleep

Physical activity and general fitness are two of the factors which contribute to a healthy lifestyle, a third one is sleep. Swimming teachers/coaches should be mindful of the need for the appropriate amount and quality of rest and sleep. The requirements for rest and sleep differ for individual people and, therefore, it is not possible to set hard and fast rules which apply in all cases. However, there are general guidelines which may be followed in order to ensure as far as possible that an individual is getting the appropriate level of rest. A child who appears to be still tired on waking, or who yawns frequently or dozes in the early part of the day is showing the symptoms of insufficient sleep. Such a child must be encouraged to have periods of inactivity and, preferably, sleep for longer periods. Inability to sleep may be linked to an anxiety state and may not be associated with the level of physical activity of the child. Where this seems likely, the teacher/coach or parent must discuss the problem with the child using a quiet concerned approach in an attempt to discover the source of the anxiety. Frequently, anxiety in children can be associated with school and is often related to some incident which is quite insignificant to an adult.

Diet

A balanced diet is important to everyone whether they take an active part in a sporting activity or not. While high level competitive swimmers may feel the need to keep a close check on their diet and make changes to it according to the detail of their training or competition time-table, for people learning to swim a good balanced diet should suffice. To achieve this balance it is important to control within reasonable limits the intake of the three main food types, carbohydrates, proteins and fats. In addition to these main types, vitamins, mineral salts, water and roughage must also be present in the diet. Where the three major food types are consumed in the correct proportions it is likely that these other additional constituents will also be present. However, their effectiveness can depend upon whether the food, e.g., fruit, vegetables, meat, are fresh or processed before final cooking and, on the manner of the cooking.

- ● **Carbohydrates** – the main source of energy for the body is obtained from carbohydrates which are found in starchy and sugary foods. The bulk of carbohydrate intake should preferably be made up of starchy or complex carbohydrates such as pasta, bread, potatoes and pulses since they release their energy over a longer period of time and, also, contain essential vitamins and minerals. Sugary foods or simple carbohydrates should be kept to a minimum. However, since the complex form of carbohydrate tends also to be bulky, swimmers training for competition will need to take account of this in their energy intake. Where the consumption of carbohydrates is too high, the body stores the surplus under the skin in the form of fat.
- ● **Proteins** – the body requires protein for replacement of tissues worn out by normal body processes. In addition, children need a significant amount of protein to foster normal healthy growth. The

important constituents of protein are the amino-acids, all of which can be obtained from eating a mixture of animal proteins, e.g., meat, fish, eggs, cheese, milk and/or vegetable protein, e.g., pulse vegetables and nuts.

● **Fats** – the body stores energy in the form of fat. Although some fat is essential in the diet to provide the fat-soluble vitamins A and D and fatty acids, it is the least essential of the three food types and its intake should be kept under strict control to avoid the risk of heart disease. Fat is also a much more concentrated energy source than protein or carbohydrate, so even small amounts are high in calories.

The proportions of the three food types necessary for a balanced diet are affected to some extent by occupation and lifestyle but, in general terms, approximately 55% to 60% of the normal intake should consist of carbohydrate, and 30% fats. The rest, i.e., 10%-15%, being made up of protein.

Figure 5.1 Comparative nutrient content of three snack meals

Snack meal	√Best choice	Content	WT g	Energy kJ kcal	Carbohydrate g	Carbohydrate % energy	Protein g	Protein % energy	Fat g	Fat % energy	Calcium mg	Iron mg	Vit C mg	Vit B$_1$ mg
1	√	Jacket potato Cheddar cheese	150 25	898 kJ 219 kcal	27	46% (complex)	10.2	19%	8.5	35%	206	0.7	11.0	0.31
		Milk chocolate	50g	1107 kJ 264 kcal	30	43% (simple)	4.2	6%	15.1	51%	110	0.8	—	—
2	√	2 slices w'meal toast Baked beans	50g 100g	800 kJ 188 kcal	35.9	72% (complex)	9.3	20%	1.8	8%	75	2.7	—	0.25
		Ice cream, dairy	100g	691 kJ 165 kcal	20.7	47% (simple)	3.3	8%	8.2	45%	120	0.3	—	0.15
3	√	Beefburger Bun (white) Orange	50g 50g 100g	1720kJ 408 kcal	41.3	39% (mostly complex)	24.1	25%	15.6	36%	103	2.6	50	0.2
		Chocolate cake with butter icing	75g	1569 kJ 375 kcal	39.8	40% (simple)	4.3	5%	23.2	55%	97	1.2	—	—

Safety

Following the publication of *Safety in Swimming Pools* (see Part V), in the Spring of 1988, greater emphasis has been placed on the safe use of pools. Paragraphs 189 to 197 of the Report explain in some detail the level of training recommended for lifeguards, and suggests that all those involved in the teaching/coaching of swimming are strongly advised to hold a lifeguarding qualification appropriate to their level of duty and responsibility in the pool environment. For those whose duties are restricted to being responsible for a group of people during programmed swimming sessions the ASA and RLSS recommend their Joint Lifesaving Certificate as the appropriate qualification. However, those who provide a comprehensive lifeguarding service should seek to gain the RLSS Pool Lifeguard Bronze Medallion as their minimum qualification. It is important to appreciate that under the Health and Safety at Work Act, the pool owner is ultimately responsible for the level of safety cover at the pool. Local authorities interpret this responsibility differently and, therefore, the lifeguarding requirements for pools in neighbouring authorities may be significantly different. As a consequence it is essential that swimming teachers/coaches, whether paid or voluntary, are aware of the particular interpretation of the Health and Safety Guidelines in force at any pool where they work, and that they hold the appropriate qualification for lifesaving. In most cases, this qualification is likely to be a current award issued by the RLSS, but some authorities have their own testing arrangements. Although *Safety in Swimming Pools* is issued for guidance purposes to pool owners and users, it is likely that, in any case involving litigation, the court would seek to establish whether its recommendations were being met in the circumstances under investigation. The extent to which the guidelines were being met might prove to be an important factor in the deliberations and subsequent outcome of the case.

The ASA strongly recommends all swimming teachers and coaches involved in any facet of the sport to gain, and keep up-to-date, a lifesaving qualification. Swimming clubs are advised to monitor continuously the level of lifesaving expertise of their teachers and coaches. Clubs affiliated to the ASA have an exceptionally good safety record which can only be maintained by constant vigilance and adherence to the local interpretation of the guidelines.

From what has been stated previously it will be obvious that, during any activity taking place in a swimming pool, the safety of the class must take priority over all other considerations. For example, if the depth of water is not adequate for diving practices to be carried out safely by novices from the poolside, a teacher/coach would be ill-advised to use such practices with a class. The ASA recommends that novices learning to perform head first entries from the poolside should do so in a **minimum** depth of water at least equal to the full stretch height (arms and fingers extended above the head) of the performer, or 1.8 metres, whichever is the greater.

Safety in swimming pools is a matter of discipline and training for both the teacher/coach and the taught. Teachers/coaches must ensure that they are familiar with the emergency procedure of the pool and that the safety equipment is accessible and in good working order. A well organised establishment will have details of its emergency procedure clearly visible to all who teach and coach. Such procedures should include the following as a minimum, but must be adapted to the provisions of the pool:

- location of emergency signal, e.g., bell push
- location of rescue equipment, e.g., poles, ropes
- location of first aid kit including resuscitation equipment
- location of superviser on duty
- location of nearest available telephone with outside line
- telephone number of accident/emergency service

In addition, there must always be someone on duty who is familiar with the correct working of all available emergency equipment. As an added precaution on safety, swimming teachers/coaches might usefully consider the advantage of carrying, as part of their personal equipment, some form of rescue line which can be placed on the pool-side behind where they are working. A weighted line (i.e., one with a cylindrical or spherical floating object on one end) will be sufficient for the majority of emergency cases in a pool, especially if it is supplemented by poles of one to two metres length for reaching rescues.

Dry Rescue Techniques

As a matter of principle, swimming teachers/coaches should avoid going into the water in an emergency. This will reduce the risk of the teacher/coach getting into difficulties and permits a measure of control to be maintained over the rest of the class. However, where essential for the saving of life, the teacher/coach must be prepared to go in the water and effect a rescue. Obviously these dry rescue techniques may only be employed when the victim is conscious.

- **Reaching Rescue** – a reaching rescue is both safe for the rescuer and effective for the victim. It is particularly effective for weak or non-swimmers who are in difficulties close to the pool-side. The rescue aids used may be rigid, e.g., a pole, or non-rigid, e.g. a towel. To perform a reaching rescue a few simple rules should be followed. The rescuer should:
    - attract the victim's attention and give reassurance
    - keep his centre of gravity as low as possible
    - keep the victim under close observation
    - attain a comfortable secure position, if necessary a helper can hold the rescuer's legs
    - reach out with the aid and tell the victim to grab hold of it
    - haul the victim to safety with a steady movement

If as a result of the victim's panic, there is a risk of the rescuer being pulled into the water, the aid should be released.

- **A throwing rescue** – if a rope weighted by a floating object (e.g., plastic bottle) is used it can generally be thrown with greater accuracy. In order to perform successfully the rescuer should:
    - attract the victim's attention and give re-assurance
    - tell the victim to expect something to be thrown
    - avoid standing too close to the edge of the pool
    - coil and throw the rope
    - instruct the victim to hold the rope with both hands
    - haul in the rope using a steady (not necessarily quick) hand over hand action
    - help the victim out of the water if necessary

Figure 5.2 Reaching rescue – rigid rescue aid.

Right: Figure 5.4 Throwing rescue.

Below: Figure 5.3 Reaching rescue – non-rigid rescue aid.

It is important to establish with classes of children a clearly understood code of discipline which applies whenever they visit the swimming pool. The reasons for various safety measures can make an interesting topic for a classroom discussion, preferably before the children make their first formal visit to the pool. This may require close co-operation between the swimming teacher/coach and the class teacher where these are not the same person. Topics which may be discussed include the following:

● Why are drinks in glass bottles not allowed in the changing rooms?
● Why should you visit the toilet before going in the pool?
● Why should you not eat sweets or chew gum when going into the pool?
● Why must you blow your nose just before you go swimming?
● Why should you use the shower and footbath before going into the pool?
● Why should you have a shower before getting dry?
● Why must you make sure you are completely dry before dressing?

It is equally important that a safe routine is followed when children leave the changing room. This should start with the teacher counting the number of pupils in a class before they go on to the poolside. The group must clearly understand that no-one enters the water without direct permission from the teacher. Once in the water a partner "check" system works well, especially with large classes. The children each have a partner and are "responsible" for checking on them regularly. It is preferable if the partners are already good friends. This is often known as the "Buddy" system.

The class discipline procedure in the pool must include a code of signals with which all children are familiar, and to which they react without undue delay. Obviously a simple system is best and might involve:

● a single blast on the whistle meaning stop and listen
● a double blast meaning clear the pool quickly

However, it should be appreciated that children below the age of about eight years may not act rationally in a real emergency situation.

Throughout their education in swimming and associated water activities children must be made aware of the dangers as well as the joys of being in water. From an early age they should be acquainted with a list of "do's" and "dont's" for safety in a pool. Nowadays most pools have notices illustrating activities which are not permitted on safety grounds, but it is the teachers'/coaches' responsibility to ensure that children understand **why** the activities are not permitted (especially those which appear to be great fun). Actions which should not be allowed in swimming pools include the following:

- running on the poolside
- pushing others into the water
- ducking
- jumping into a crowded area
- throwing swimming aids
- vigorous splashing

When meeting children for the first time in a swimming pool it is essential that teachers check on the swimming ability of their charges. They should not be misled by rows of badges on swim-wear or by a verbal description of swimming prowess. All descriptions of swimming ability coming from young children should be treated with caution; the definition of "a good swimmer" is capable of wide interpretation.

Medical considerations

Hygiene and related medical topics can be usually discussed with children away from the poolside and before their first lesson. Although it is sufficient for them to be given a list of "do's" and "don'ts" on the subject it is far better if they do understand **why** they are not allowed in the pool under certain circumstances. Opinions on whether children should swim while suffering from certain common medical conditions vary and, therefore, where there is any doubt, professional advice should be sought from a family doctor or school nurse. It is preferable to exclude the child from swimming until medical advice has been obtained rather than risk additional complications. There are, however, some generally accepted conditions which should lead to exclusion. These include:

- infectious diseases
- open wounds
- coughs, colds and related infections such as catarrh, sinusitis
- sore eyes
- ear infections

The two main conditions which give rise to differences of view on their treatment are Verrucae (Plantar warts) and Athlete's Foot. Verrucae are infectious warts on the soles of the feet which, if identified at an early stage, can be cleared up quickly before they become painful. They are readily transmitted at swimming pools through contact between the feet and damp surfaces. One view is that they should be cleared up before swimming resumes, but the more modern view is that swimming may continue provided the infected area is covered by an appropriate "sock". Athlete's foot is caused by a fungus which infects the skin, particularly between the smaller toes, and gives rise to reddening, irritation and scaling of the infected area. The infection is carried by the skin scales which are deposited on the floor and picked up by another person. Special anti-fungal powders are available to treat the condition which will usually clear up quickly. Again however, one view is that swimming may continue provided the infected foot is covered by an impervious sock. The alternate view is that swimming should cease until the infection has been cleared up.

Chapter 6

Elementary Exercise Physiology
Mike Seddon

Introduction

A swimmer is like other athletes in that a well-planned and lengthy period of training is essential in order to reach the necessary level of physical fitness, and so help to bring about swimming success and enjoyment. This training can be complex and should be monitored by a qualified and experienced teacher/coach, who will have undergone the practical and theoretical preparation necessary to apply the latest training theory. The training will have a seasonal element to it, as well as a variety of appropriate work that will need to be done to establish a balanced and broad physical preparation to meet the requirements of the specific swimmer.

While swimming is a most attractive pastime, with its cardiovascular benefits being promoted for health and general fitness, it is at the same time one of the most physiologically exacting sports. Consequently, teachers/coaches should be constantly alert so that the needs and individual differences of their swimmers can be taken into account.

The Physical Effects of Exercise

In Chapter 5 reference was made to the "3Ss". A fourth "S", Speed, might also be added. For all-round fitness an individual should possess an adequate amount of each by ensuring that all the components are included in their exercise programme on a regular basis. Simply by swimming regularly, suppleness, strength and stamina will be improved. However, the demands of a serious competitive programme will need a much more detailed and structured approach than just simply swimming regularly. Chapter 7 deals with the training process in detail.

Warm-up

A warm-up should be done before any strenuous swimming session. This can be done on land, or in the water. Warm-up increases the body temperature, which helps to increase the speed of the energy-releasing reactions in the muscles. Blood is diverted to the exercising muscles away from other parts of the body. The blood vessels leading to the muscles become enlarged (dilated), increasing the supply of blood and, consequently, the oxygen supply from the blood to the muscle is also increased. Benefits of warm-up include:

- warmer muscles which contract and relax more easily and faster than cold muscles
- reduction of soft tissue injury (muscle tear; ligament or tendon rupture)
- less likelihood of abnormal electrical activity in the heart
- faster nerve impulse travel

If done in the water, the warm-up could consist of swimming the first few lengths slowly and then gradually increasing the pace.

Cooling-down

At the end of a vigorous swimming session a cooling down procedure, often called "warming" or "swimming down", is a sound practice. Even mild muscular action can help the return of blood to the heart and, therefore, assist in the removal of lactic acid and other waste products. Recovery, therefore, will be aided if it is in an active, rather than passive form.

Suppleness

Suppleness, which is also known as flexibility or mobility, is important as a lack of it limits the range of movement of the joints thereby affecting swimming speed and efficiency. Suppleness may be lost through inactivity. A good level of suppleness can reduce the risk of stiffness or injury which can occur during strenuous swimming. Flexibility depends upon the bone structure of the joint, and the ligaments, muscles and tendons surrounding the joint capsule. Flexibility exercises should safely increase the range of movement by gentle stretching over the full range of the particular joint and holding the position. Using slow smooth actions, as opposed to jerking or bouncing movements, will ensure that the muscles and tendons can stretch fully. Limiting factors on joint mobility are:

- type of joint
- tension in the muscles surrounding the joint
- ligaments supporting the joint
- speed of movement
- tissue and environmental temperature
- training and condition of the joint

Muscular Strength and Endurance

The voluntary or skeletal muscles which move the swimmer through the water make up approximately 45% of body weight and consist largely of protein. They are attached to bone at both ends by very strong non-stretchable fibres. Muscle tissue is made up of many bundles of fibres which, when activated by a nervous impulse, become shorter and thicker. Each muscle fibre either contracts completely or remains at rest, often referred to as the "all or none" response. Fibres cannot contract partially but, within a single muscle, some fibres may be contracted while others are relaxed. In any muscle there are always some fibres in a state of contraction. This is known as "muscle tone", which is a characteristic of all healthy muscles and holds them in a state of readiness for action. When these contracted fibres begin to fatigue, others will contract to maintain the tension.

There are several types of muscle fibre the characteristics of which are usually classified into two groups, fast and slow twitch. The fast-twitch (FT) fibres are used for short, sharp bursts of activity and can work without oxygen (anaerobically), and would be particularly involved in sprint swimming. The slow-twitch (ST) fibres are best suited for endurance swimming as these have a high capacity for taking up and using oxygen (working aerobically). Sprinters are likely to have a rather higher proportion of FT fibres, with endurance swimmers having a higher proportion of ST fibres. Muscles usually work in groups. As one group of muscles (known as agonists or originators) contracts to bring about a movement, others (antagonists) relax to enable it to take place in a controlled manner. Other muscle groups may be working simultaneously (known as reciprocal innervation) to prevent unwanted and unnecessary movements.

The swimmer needs great muscular force and anaerobic power for fast propulsion through the water. In distances greater than 100m, the aerobic capacity and muscular endurance are emphasised. The muscle power of the arms and shoulders is particularly important in sprint swimming. Other muscle groups are called upon depending on the stroke and on the leg kick pattern. The muscles of the trunk are of particular importance as stabilizers in the maintenance of a streamlined posture. The maximum force that a muscle can develop depends on:

- the size of the muscle (the area of the muscle's largest cross-section)
- the skill and co-ordination level for that particular movement
- the length of the muscle during the movement
- the speed at which the muscle shortens (contracts)

An improvement in strength can be achieved by a variety of methods. Each should involve "progressive over-load". The exercise can be either "dynamic" or "static". In dynamic, or "isotonic", exercise the limbs are moved against a load, and positions held only briefly, so that the blood flow is maintained and adaptations to the fibres can occur. The greatest strength gains are made when the intensity of the contraction is over 80% of the muscle's own maximum, which is usually when approximately only ten repetitions of the exercise can be done. The term "over-load" is used here to mean exercising the muscle progressively near its limit. Static (isometric) muscle contraction, when the muscle contracts without movement at a joint, can bring out strength gains, but is not as suitable for swimmers.

As the muscle becomes stronger:

- the connective tissue, tendons and ligaments surrounding joints become stronger, making it more stable
- muscle fibres become thicker which allows the muscles to pull more powerfully
- there are more enzymes to help the release of energy without oxygen (anaerobically)
- the swimmer's body gains a higher proportion of muscle and a lower proportion of fat tissue than the population at large
- blood capillaries increase in number and are found closer to muscle fibres

Cardiovascular Respiratory System

Stamina, otherwise known as endurance, is the ability to keep going, and is a vital factor in the physical fitness of swimmers. When exercising, the activity of the muscles requires an increase in their metabolism (the process of breaking down and releasing energy).

A muscle contraction, be it strong or weak, is as a result of a complex chemical chain reaction, culminating in work (in this case swimming) being done. The energy for this work is chemical energy contained in high energy phosphate compounds, notably adenosine triphosphate (ATP), within the muscles. ATP is the body's main source of energy for muscular contraction since it is a compound held together with high energy bonds. The breaking of one of these bonds, when a phosphate group is split off the ATP molecule, releases energy for muscular contraction.

A-P-P-P(ATP) ....A-P-P(ADP [adenosine diphosphate]) + P + Energy (used for muscular contraction)

Unfortunately, the store of ATP within the muscles can be used up in 2 seconds unless it is replaced in some way. To maintain muscular activity in the muscles used in swimming, it is essential that ATP is produced and the depleted stores of the compound are replenished. There are three energy pathways which allow this production and replenishment to take place: anaerobic alactic; anaerobic lactate; aerobic.

Anaerobic alactic energy system

An energy rich compound in the muscle known as creatine phosphate (CP) provides the immediate source of energy for the resynthesis of ATP. A transfer of a phosphate group (P) from CP to ADP produces the necessary ATP. The process can then repeat itself when once again the ATP is broken down into ADP with the release of further energy. When the exercise is intense, this process will continue until the CP stores are depleted.

ADP + CP ....ATP + C

ATP ....ADP + P + Energy for swimming

Resynthesis of ATP in this manner can only last for 4 to 5 seconds when swimming at maximum effort. When the 1 to 2 seconds of energy which is initially available in the muscle is added to this, it is seen that approximately 7 seconds of ATP production is possible. This is the anaerobic (without oxygen) alactic (without lactate) energy system when swimming occurs at a high intensity and speed for very short periods without a build-up of lactate and hydrogen ions (sometimes referred to as lactic acid).

Anaerobic Lactate Energy System

The intensity and duration of the swim and, therefore, the demand for energy (ATP), will determine which of the two other energy systems is challenged. The anaerobic lactate energy system involves the breakdown of glucose or glycogen anaerobically (without oxygen) to produce energy plus lactate plus hydrogen ions (H+).

Glucose + 2P + 2ADP ...2ATP + 2 Lactate + 2(H+)

When glucose is used 2ATP molecules are produced, and when glycogen is used 3 ATP molecules are produced. The accumulation of hydrogen ions is a limiting factor when exercising without oxygen and the body will be fatigued after 40 to 50 seconds of all-out effort. Therefore, for efforts of greater duration the aerobic energy system is used.

Aerobic Energy System

In the aerobic system, pyruvate (from glucose and glycogen) and fatty acids (from stored fats) are oxidised (i.e., using oxygen), via an intermediate stage, to carbon dioxide and water. Since, as the term implies, oxygen must be available, this energy system is named the "aerobic" system. It is the availability of oxygen in the muscle cell which determines to what extent the process is aerobic or anaerobic. This energy system is particularly suitable for swims when the intensity of the effort is approximately 40 to 60 percent of maximum and, therefore, the pace can be maintained for some considerable time. For swimming to continue for any extended length of time, therefore, the metabolism has to be at least partially aerobic, and the supply of oxygen must meet the demand created for:

● energy release
● waste disposal

Blood Circulation

The heart, lungs and blood vessels are the main organs involved in this process. The heart is a muscular pump and is divided into two distinct halves. Each half pumps to a separate system. The right side pumps the blood through the pulmonary system, i.e., to the lungs, where it is oxygenated, to be returned to the left side whence it is pumped around the systemic circulation carrying blood to the remaining organs and tissues of the body. At the tissues, and during exercise this particularly means the muscles, oxygen passes from the blood through the thin-walled capillaries, and the now oxygen-deficient blood, containing waste products, such as lactate and carbon dioxide, flows back to the right side of the heart for subsequent pumping to the lungs for re-oxygenation and removal of the excess carbon dioxide.

Figure 6.1 The heart.

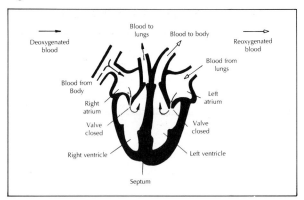

Figure 6.2 The blood circulation.

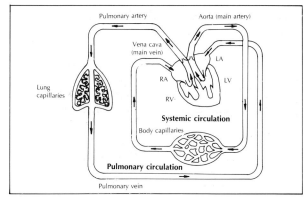

Breathing

The oxygen reaches the lungs via the mechanism of breathing. The main organs involved in breathing are the trachea, the left and right bronchus (one to each lung), bronchioles and alveoli (air-sacs). As air enters the nasal passages it is warmed to body temperature, humidified and filtered by small hairs and mucus.

The lungs and heart are contained inside the chest or thorax. The internal surface of the thoracic cavity and the outer surfaces of the lungs are lined by the pleura, a double layer of membrane, containing a fluid which acts as a lubricant. The expansion and contraction of the lungs which allows air to enter (inhalation) or leave (exhalation) is caused by the muscular movements of the thoracic boundaries. This results in a difference in air pressure between the inside of the lungs and the thoracic cavity so that the pressure in the lungs is always higher. This higher lung pressure has two very important effects:

Figure 6.3 The lungs.

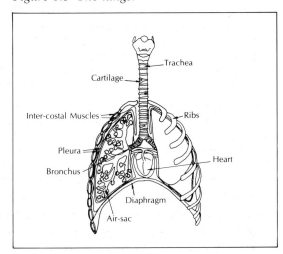

- it causes the walls of the alveoli to stretch so that the lungs almost fill the thoracic cavity completely
- it ensures that during breathing, when the volume of the thoracic cavity increases, the lungs inflate to fill all the available space completely

The increase in volume of the thoracic cavity is caused by changes in the intercostal muscles and a dome-shaped muscle at the bottom of the cavity called the diaphragm.

Although individuals can control breathing rate and the volume of air being moved, there are times when breathing is a reflex action, i.e., occurs automatically, and is beyond the control of individuals. During an energetic swimming session the level of carbon dioxide (CO_2) in the blood rises because of the increased production of this gas in the muscle tissues. The nerve endings in the walls of some arteries react to this increased carbon dioxide concentration and cause impulses to be sent to the respiratory centres of the brain which result in an automatic increase in the depth and rate of breathing.

Figure 6.4 The action of the diaphragm.

Figure 6.5 The movement of the thoracic wall.

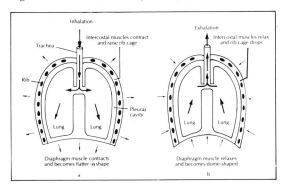

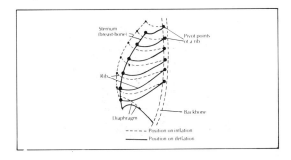

Cardiovascular respiratory system during exercise

During vigorous activity the muscles need an increased supply of fuel and oxygen. To achieve this more blood must be pumped to the muscles, and at the same time re-directed away (shunted) from organs not essential to exercise such as the gut, kidneys and skin. This is why it is usually unwise to exercise very vigorously immediately after a heavy meal. In addition to the blood shunt, the circulation is increased by:

- the active muscles producing a larger venous return
- lower thoracic pressure facilitating the venous return
- the increase in the volume of blood returning to the heart causes stretching of its muscle fibres. The more the heart expands and stretches, the greater the subsequent contraction pumping more blood around the body per stroke (stroke/volume).

The elevated levels of carbon dioxide in the blood will increase the rate of the heart beat as well as affecting breathing. When there has been an increased level of demand for oxygen, as there will be in vigorous swimming, after two or three minutes the heart rate settles down to a steady state (homeostasis), where oxygen and fuel supply equals demand. If demand cannot be met then the body gradually runs into debt. This state is called "oxygen debt". An increase in the rate and depth of breathing after finishing a swim is a way of repaying the muscles the oxygen they had required during exercise. The swimmer can increase his lactate tolerance with training, thereby further improving stamina.

To summarise, the oxygen requirements of exercising muscle are met by cardiovascular changes:

- increase in cardiac output reflected in an increase in heart rate and stroke/volume
- re-distribution (shunting) of blood from relatively inactive tissues to the muscles
- increase in the ability of muscle cells to extract and use oxygen

Chapter 7

Principles and Types of Training
Cliff Dedynski

Introduction

Whether designing a single lesson or a four year training programme culminating in the Olympics, the teacher/coach must be aware of certain fundamental "training principles". These principles must be incorporated into the different types of training and this chapter is designed to:

- help the teacher/coach understand how he can apply those principles when constructing his schedules and work loads
- introduce some of the different types of training and give examples of typical sets

Training Principles

Traditionally, coaching manuals and swimming books refer to "the three overriding principles" which must be complied with if the training programme is to be effective – namely, specificity, overload and progression. However in this analysis of training principles a broader view will be taken and a total of seven principles will be introduced:

- Overload
- Progressive overload
- Adaptation
- Specificity
- Underloading
- Reversibility
- Motivation

Overload

Overload is usually defined as subjecting a swimmer to a workload greater than that to which his body is accustomed. Unless the coach insists on such a workload it is highly unlikely that, other things remaining equal, there will be any improvement in performance at all. In fact, a poorly designed schedule may include no overload and, therefore, result in a loss of aerobic and anaerobic capacity which, at best, may result in simply maintaining current fitness levels. Good training programmes, however, include overload in three ways:

- **frequency** – the number of sessions per day or per week. For example, in early season (September/October) the young age-groupers may only train 2 or 3 times per week. As the season progresses the number of sessions may be increased gradually to 5 or 6 per week, and when the swimmers go on training camps they may find themselves doing 10 or 11 sessions in a week!
- **duration** – how long each session lasts. Again this may be increased gradually as the swimmers conditioning improves, say, from perhaps 30/45 minutes to 2/2½ hours. Again, this is often associated with progress through the season.

● **intensity** – the training loads imposed on the swimmer within each schedule. The most important factors here would be speed, rest interval and number of repetitions. There is an increasing amount of evidence which suggests that all swimmers should do 80% to 90% of their training on, or just under, their anaerobic threshold. This will be explained a little later. As regards overloading, it is essential that the intensity be sufficient, and this means that the swimmer must swim at the optimum velocity for that particular type of training. Training too fast (overtraining) or training too slow (undertraining) for too much of the available time will result in a deterioration in the swimmer's performances. This is further explained when the types of training are introduced.

Progressive overload

Even if the body is subjected to overload in the first week or two of a programme it will soon adapt to that workload – more muscle fibres will have been used and the circulatory system will have become better at distributing more blood and oxygen to the muscles needing it, etc. Consequently, the swimmer will no longer be in a state of overload and it will become necessary to change the training target times, or reduce the rest intervals or increase the number of repetitions. These regular adjustments result in progressive overload and ensure that the swimmer continues to adapt to ever greater and more challenging workloads.

Adaptation

Imposing the optimum workload for each individual swimmer will result in optimum adaptation. However the teacher/coach must bear two factors in mind when making these adjustments to the training programme. Firstly, adaptation is very individual and some swimmers will adapt more quickly than others. This should be taken into account when setting, and then adjusting individual training target times. It will sometimes result in swimmers having to move up or down a training lane. Secondly, failing adaptation will result if the process of progressive overload is pushed too hard too soon, i.e., before the swimmer has adapted to the current workloads. The teacher/coach must always be sensitive to such failure and be able to identify the signs of failing adaptation. These signs are:
● injuries – especially to the knee joint and to the shoulder
● stroke breakdown – a very common problem, and often associated with, for example, too much full stroke Butterfly before the swimmer is ready
● illness – often a result of the swimmer being overstressed by an excessive workload
● demotivation – the end result of injuries, illness, loss of stroke and deteriorating performances in both training and competition. If not spotted in time the swimmer will drop out.

Given the very serious consequences of failing to recognise "failing adaptation" it is one of the key responsibilities of a sensitive, observant teacher/coach. Remedial measures would involve a reduced, manageable workload, more rest and lots of reassurance. Confidence has to be rebuilt.

Underloading (easier than reality)

Sometimes it is important to deliberately "underload" swimmers. The classic example is drills based on swim fins. Fins take much of the workload off swimmers and allow them to concentrate on their stroke development. This is particularly beneficial when teaching/coaching Butterfly, but useful for all strokes – even Breaststroke, e.g., Dolphin leg kick, Breaststroke arm pulling. Swim fins are also used for "speed assistance" type training, i.e., the swimmers can swim faster with less effort. Consequently, they enjoy the sensation of "feeling fast" in the water and this can have beneficial psychological effects. Finally, operating in the "underload zone" is often built into schedules in order to allow swimmers to warm up, or to recover more quickly between hard swims or sets. This is sometimes called "active rest" and is designed to reduce lactate levels and get rid of any oxygen debt.

Specificity

The human body will make specific adaptations to specific types of training. An understanding of the principle of "training specificity" is important and forms the foundation on which a well-balanced programme of the various types of training can be built. Training specificity means that each type of training has a specific effect and, therefore, the teacher/coach must design an overall package which includes elements of all the major types of training – threshold training, lactate tolerance training, speed training, etc. All these terms are explained below.

Reversibility

The benefits of training do not last for ever and are easily lost. Research suggests that endurance can be lost in one third of the time it took to achieve it. *(Body in Action – NCF Introductory Study pack 2*, see reference section page 158). Muscles wither more slowly, but any muscle will atrophy (reduce in size/mass) if it is not used. Training adaptations are, therefore, lost if there is a prolonged lay off. What, then, is a "prolonged" lay off, and how can the loss of conditioning be minimized? Taking an annual break of 3 or 4 weeks is bordering on "prolonged" but much depends on what the swimmers are doing during the lay off. If they are confined to bed for two or three weeks then research suggests that it will take something like twice as long to regain the conditioning lost. (Saltin, Blomquist et al, *Responses to Submaximal and Maximal Exercises after Bedrest and training*, Circulation 38, supp. 7, 1968). However, if the swimmers are encouraged to be active in their annual break then the loss of condition will not be so serious. Running, cycling, circuit training and rowing all help to maintain swimmers' endurance and, to an extent, their strength. Although reversibility may have to be taken into account when swimmers come back after illness or injury it is still important that swimmers are encouraged to take an annual break. It recharges the mental batteries for the whole of the next season and is well worth the slight loss of conditioning.

Motivation

Motivation is probably the most important of all training principles. Without it the teacher/coach is doomed to failure and swimmers will drop out. The good teacher/coach will nearly always be a good psychologist and good motivator. A motivating training programme will provide for:

● setting "goals", i.e., training target times, competition targets, perhaps a "total meterage" target, etc. These give the swimmers an added sense of purpose, and they like hitting targets.

● variety, i.e., stimulate interest by "ringing the changes", e.g., a hard session followed by an easy relaxed session. Always doing the same "speed" session on a Wednesday evening can become too predictable and lacks imagination. Keep the swimmers guessing a little.

● "Always finishing on a high", an old saying, but still a good one. It is important to remember one of Thorndike's laws of learning theory;

"We tend to repeat a pleasant experience and avoid an unpleasant one."

The swimmers will remember the last set particularly vividly, especially if it is good fun and a pleasant experience.

Types of Training

The Endurance/Speed continuum

Although there are many types of training – interval training, fartlek training, hypoxic training, threshold training, etc, they are all built into a programme in order to improve either the "endurance" or the "speed" of the swimmers involved. There is general agreement now that all training programmes should be endurance based, whether for age groupers, seniors, long distance freestylers or for sprinters. Speed or "power" training should not be ignored but it should only make up 3% to 10% of the programme. Endurance type training will make up 90% plus of a typical, scientifically designed swim programme. Some of the different types of training are summarized in Fig. 7.1.

Figure 7.1 Summary of different types of training

Aerobic endurance (80%+)			Anaerobic endurance (5%)		Speed (5%)
Type of training	Basic endurance	Overload endurance	VO_2	Lactate tolerance	Speed training
Pulse	130-170	170-200	Maximum – 10	Maximum	Maximum
Set length	20-30 mins	10-15 mins	10-20 mins	500-1000 metres	300-600 metres
Work/		Ratio 1:1	Ratio 2:1	Ratio 1:3	Ratio 1:5
Rest	15-45 secs	Work 2 mins	Work 3 mins	Work 40 secs	Work 10 secs
Guide	per repeat	Rest 2 mins	Rest 1.5 mins	Rest 2 mins	Rest 50 secs
Typical set	10×100 FC	5×200 No. 1 stroke	3×300 FC	10×50 No. 1 stroke	6×25 No. 1 stroke
	With 30 secs	With 2 mins	On 5 mins	On 2 mins	On 1m 30 secs

Note 1. The above table is a set of guidelines only and must be used as such. Some of the work-rest ratios and set lengths will have to be adjusted according to the ability and fitness of the swimmers being coached.

Note 2. Use of pulse – the pulse should be taken immediately on cessation of the exercise for 6 seconds, e.g., pulse of 18 in 6 seconds = 180 per minute.

Note 3. The remaining 5%-10% of training would be made up of warm up, recovery swimming (swimming of down) and drills.

Interval Training

This has now become the dominant form of training and is the staple diet of all modern training programmes. As its name suggests, it involves swimming a given number of repeats (R) at a particular target time (TT) and with a specific rest interval (With 30 seconds – or "On" a 2 minute turn round).

Example 1

Swim 10 × 100 Front Crawl (FC) With (w) 30 seconds rest. A suggested target time (TT) might be 1m 10 secs. Here there are 10 repetitions, the distance being swum is 100 metres each time, the rest interval is 30 seconds and the training target time is 1m 10 seconds.

This will result in a total of about 12-15 minutes work at the prescribed pace and should overload the swimmer involved. As the season progresses, and the swimmer becomes better conditioned, this set would have to be adjusted, otherwise the swimmer would no longer be overloaded and would not improve. Progressive overload would, therefore, suggest that one of the variables must be changed.

Example 2
Swim 10 × 100 FC With (w) 30 seconds. TT 1m 08 seconds
or   12 × 100 FC w 30 seconds. TT 1m 10 seconds
or   10 × 100 FC w 20 seconds. TT 1m 10 seconds

Each of the three adjustments comply with the progressive overload principle. The swimmers usually find such adjustments both challenging and motivating, provided that the new "goals" are realistic and achievable.

Example 3
Swim 12 × 50 No. 1 stroke. On 1 minute. TT = 50% of 100 metres Personal Best (PB).

Threshold Training (80% to 90% of total training) Basic and Overload Endurance
This is a type of aerobic (with oxygen) endurance training in which the swimmer is taking in just enough oxygen to meet the energy demands of his body. As indicated in Fig. 7.1, the pulse would normally be in the region of 140-190 beats per minute depending on the individual swimmer and how close to the threshold the swimmer is training. Given that the great majority of training should be close to this threshold it is important to lay down guidelines and give examples which can be used when designing schedules. There seems to be general agreement that swimmers should train at about 75% to 85% of race pace based on PB and that pulse rates of 140-180 beats per minutes would indicate that such speeds were being achieved. Faster speeds should not be encouraged when doing this type of training

Example 1
Charlie has a freestyle PB of 60 seconds. His 80% pace would therefore be 60 + 20% of 60 = 60 + 12 = 1m 12 secs. A threshold set for Charlie would therefore be:
10 × 100 Freestyle w 30 seconds. TT = 1m 12 seconds.

Example 2
Jo has a Back Crawl PB of 1m 20 seconds. Her 80% pace would be 1m 36 seconds (80 + 20% of 80). A threshold set for her would be:
10 × 100 Back Crawl w 30 seconds. TT = 1m 36 seconds.

VO_2 or Maximum Oxygen Consumption Training (Up to 5%)
This type of training is designed to improve the swimmer's ability to absorb or consume more of the oxygen which he breathes in. The greater a swimmer's oxygen consumption capacity the better he will perform in endurance events, which means virtually all swimming events of 100 metres upwards. In order to improve our swimmer's ability to absorb oxygen refer to Fig. 7.1 again. Research suggests (Åstrand and Rodahl, *Textbook of Work Physiology*, McGraw-Hill, 1977), that the work to rest ratio should be in the order of 2:1 and that sets made up of 150 metres and 300 metres are ideal. Pace should be 80%-90% of personal best time (PB).

Example 3
Nigel has a 300m PB of 3m 30 seconds. His 90% pace is 3m 51 seconds. A VO_2 set for him would be:
4 × 300 FC. On 5m 45 seconds. TT = 3m 51 seconds.

Lactate Tolerance Training (Up to 5% of total distance)

This type of training is designed to improve a swimmer's ability to tolerate or "buffer" high levels of lactate. It is the most painful type of training and the swimmers must be highly motivated if they are to repeatedly go through the "pain barrier" and swim the set properly. The ability to tolerate high lactate levels will enable the swimmer to "bring races home" and maintain a fast, even pace, despite the "stacking" effect of gradually increasing lactate levels. By reference to Fig. 7.1 again we can see how lactate tolerance is improved. Åstrand (ibid) suggests a work/rest ratio of about 1:3 or 1:4. Sufficient rest is critical here, otherwise the swimmer will be forced to start his next swim before he is ready. This will lead to slower swimming and the high lactate levels aimed for will not be reached. The optimum speeds are 85%-95% of PB (85% early season, 95% later). No more than two such sessions are recommended per week.

Example 4

Emma's No. 1 stroke is Butterfly, and her PB is 1m 10 seconds. It is late season. Her 95% PB pace is 1m 13.5 seconds. A lactate tolerance set for her would be:

5 × 100 No. 1 (Fly) On 5.00 mins. TT 1m 13.5 seconds. With long rests it is advisable to use "active rest" rather than passive rest. This ensures faster recovery.

Example 5

5 × (100 No. 1 – hard + 100 Freestyle – easy)
On a 5 minute turn round.

Speed training (Up to 5% of total training)

This type of training is designed to improve muscular power and to improve the so called "high energy phosphate" energy system.

As indicated on Fig. 7.1 it involves "all out" swims of very short duration. 10-20 seconds only, with long, active rest periods. Work-rest ratios would be about 1:5 or 1:6 allowing for nearly complete recovery.

Example 6

Spencer is a sprint Front Crawl swimmer. His 25 PB is 12.0 seconds A "speed" set for him would be:

10 × (25 FC – all out + 25 own choice – easy). On 1m 30 seconds. No swimmer should be subjected to such sprints until they are fully warmed up, otherwise there is a high risk of injury.

PART III

FUNDAMENTALS OF SWIMMING AND STROKE ANALYSIS

Introduction to Part III

Any teacher/coach needs to become a good observer of their performers' movements. Careful observation is as important a part of the role of teacher/coach as is the ability to impart information. The elements required are not only **what** to observe, but also **how** to set about the task of actually looking.

Whilst the stroke chapters contained in a later part of the book offer some details of the process of fault finding and correcting, it is important that the general principles of movement through the water were understood. These principles allow the teacher/coach to interpret what they see and apply appropriate techniques on an individual basis, rather than try to make their swimmers fit a particular fault or correction from a list. The notion of an exhaustive and detailed list of faults to fit every swimmer might appeal to some teachers/coaches but, generally speaking, the results would be very restricting. Part III of the book, therefore, sets out to provide the fundamentals of movement in the water, together with the principles of stroke analysis and observation techniques.

Chapter 8

Fundamentals of Swimming

David Sparkes

Introduction

It is essential for a swimming teacher/coach to appreciate that everyone will move in water in a different way. As human beings we differ in flexibility, strength and natural skill. However, the underlying principle which should be appreciated is that all movement in water is governed by the basic laws of mechanics. A good understanding of these will enable the teacher/coach to analyse movements in and out of the water, evaluate more carefully those movements and take appropriate corrective action based on a sound understanding of those same mechanical principles. Sound knowledge of mechanical principles will take advantage of a swimmer's natural ability and take into account individual swimmers' anatomical differences.

Buoyancy

A teacher/coach would probably accept the concept that most people can float to some degree. A swimmer, on the other hand, may need some considerable work on confidence to accept this statement in practical terms. In order to understand why it is possible for a human being to float it is, perhaps, first best to appreciate a simple scientific term of 'density'. This is defined as the ratio of the mass (sometimes "weight" is used) of an object to its volume. In simple terms it should be appreciated that steel is more dense than wood, which in turn is more dense than polystyrene, so every substance has density and, indeed, water itself has its own density which can vary. Sea water has a greater density than fresh water.

What decides whether something will float is whether or not it has a greater density than that of water. If it has it will tend to sink, whilst if its density is less than that of water it will float. The ratio of the density of a substance to the density of water is known as the 'specific gravity'. Substances with very low densities have a tendency to have very low specific gravities and will have a tendency to float very high in the water. Substances which have a density close to that of water, that is to say, they have a specific gravity close to one, have a tendency to float low in the water. The human body has a specific gravity of about 0.97-0.98, so its density is very close to that of water and will, therefore, float very low in the water; so low in fact that only a small part of the body will be above the water level.

With the exception of fatty (adipose) tissue, the human body is composed of sinking materials, i.e., they have a density greater than that of water. However, adipose tissue will float, and it is this, coupled with the air held within the lungs, which helps humans to achieve floatation. It is this factor which causes us to float in different ways. Women, who have a tendency to have more adipose tissue on their hips and thighs than men, and can achieve a flat floating position far more easily than men. The latter have a tendency for muscular legs which often causes them to float in a vertical position and, indeed, some men will often find it virtually impossible to float except in a position a few centimetres beneath the water surface or in a vertical position.

Clearly, therefore, a swimming teacher/coach must understand that some people are being asked to achieve a great deal when attempting a flat, streamlined body position.

Figure 8.1 *The submarine with ballast tanks.*

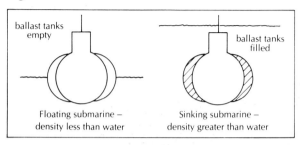

Figure 8.2 *Examples of human flotation.*

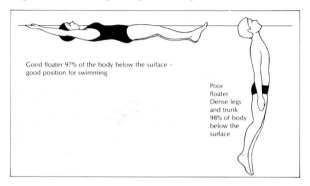

Resistance

In everyday life little thought needs to be given to the mechanical principles of walking or running. However, it is a very different matter if a runner tries to run through water. In water there are considerable forces resisting movement and a good understanding of these by a swimming teacher/coach is essential because good teaching/coaching is aimed towards minimising resistance and maximising propulsion. It may help to look at some examples of movement. If we consider a simple cylinder and a bullet, similar shaped objects in some respects, it can be noted that the larger the diameter of the cylinder the greater the resistance to forward movement of the front end. This is often referred to as profile resistance, and is a measure of the fact that resistance to forward motion increases with the size of the profile of the object. For a swimmer it is important that the frontal area which the swimmer presents to the water is kept to a minimum. Simple concepts of swimming down a tube of the smallest possible diameter may help here. Any swinging from side to side (lateral deviation), or inclination of the body in the water, should be kept to an absolute minimum as this will significantly increase profile resistance. The bullet, on the other hand, will offer less resistance than the cylinder because of its more streamlined shape whilst the cylinder must push the water away in front of it.

Movement of water has the tendency to create eddy currents which are caused by the water filling in behind the swimmer as he moves forward. This tends to pull the swimmer back, as the hole behind the swimmer needs to be filled. Turbulence is the enemy of a swimmer who wishes to move quickly through the water, and a streamlined body position offers the least turbulence; sharp changes in direction should also be avoided.

Whilst these are the main resistances which a swimmer faces there are other factors which need to be taken into account. Clearly, there is resistance to the water moving past the swimmer's body because it tends to cling. This can be greatly reduced by the use of a smooth and well fitting costume. It will also be noticed that some swimmers have a tendency to create excessive waves. Waves can be looked upon as a waste of energy and, therefore, another resistance factor. A good body position does not create excessive waves and should be encouraged. An example of this is when the swimmer pushes off under the surface in a gliding action and travels much further than when pushing off on the surface. In addition, resistance increases considerably as the speed of the swimmer increases. One of the tasks of the swimming teacher/coach is to try to ensure that such resistance is kept to a minimum.

Figure 8.3 Lateral deviation.

Figure 8.4(a) Resistance – poor body position.

Figure 8.4(b) Resistance – improved body position.

Propulsion

Our understanding of how swimmers propel themselves through water has for many years been largely based on copying the particular swimming style of a successful performer. However, in recent years a great deal of scientific study has been undertaken on what are the major factors which allow us to propel ourselves through the water. Through much improved underwater photography techniques we have come to appreciate more clearly how propulsion is achieved, and this has enabled us to modify stroke patterns by the application of sound mechanical principles. The job of a teacher/coach is to constantly analyse stroke movements and, by comparison with sound mechanical principles, to encourage swimmers to adopt patterns of movement which provide for maximum propulsion and efficiency with minimum resistance.

Travelling through the water is the result of the application of force. All forms of propulsion through a low viscosity fluid, e.g., water, involve moving some of this fluid in the opposite direction to the desired motion.

75

The paddle effect is, perhaps, the simplest way of understanding what happens. Newton's third law of motion states that for every action there is an equal and opposite reaction, e.g., if the hand pushes backwards the swimmer will travel forwards. However, if the paddle, e.g., the hand, moved in a straight line it would begin to cause a considerable mass of water to move with it, thus reducing the propulsive force generated by the hand action. By changing the path of the hand from a straight line to one that is curved, often described as "elliptical", a smaller mass of water would be moved since the hand itself is continually moving into "still" water. The result is a more efficient propulsive effect, and the swimmer travels forward further and faster. By changing the path of the hand the swimmer has taken advantage of the application of Bernoulli's "lift" theory.

Lift is based on the noted similarity between the cross section of the hand and that of an aeroplane wing. A study of the hand will show that it is flat across the palm and curved across the back of the hand. Water passing over the hand does so at different rates depending on whether it is the palm or back of the hand. Water moving across the palm of the hand has a shorter route than the water passing across the back of the hand. This produces a lower pressure on the back of the hand, relative to that on the palm, which in turn leads to lift. A simple example of the application of lift would be sculling, which does not employ any paddle effect at all. The same principle can also be applied to movements of the feet. Further detailed discussion of the application of Bernoulli lift principle is beyond the scope of the level of this book.

Figure 8.5 Action-Reaction – canoe paddle.

Figure 8.7 Airflow over a wing.

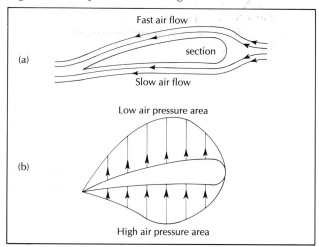

Figure 8.6 Action-Reaction – swimmer's hands.

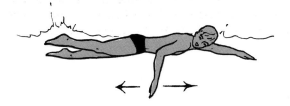

Figure 8.8 Elliptical pathways.

It would be virtually impossible to evolve at this stage an ideal stroke pattern for all swimmers. That is why the importance of observing a swimmer carefully to evaluate their stroke is followed up in Chapter 9. It is the task of the teacher/coach to understand the importance of lift and paddle and how propulsion is gained, and to encourage the swimmer to constantly strive for the "feel" of the water throughout the stroke from the catch through to the final explosive release. This will be achieved by correct pitch of the hand throughout the stroke, which the swimmer must experiment with for himself together with feedback from the teacher/coach.

Inertia

The concept of inertia is, perhaps, easier to understand if one considers the difficulty of pushing a large garden roller. The heavy object is difficult to get started, but once moving it is a relatively easy job to keep it moving but becomes a more difficult job to stop it. This initial acceleration from rest to movement is often referred to as overcoming (initial) inertia. In mechanical terms it is accepted that it requires considerable force to accelerate an object from rest up to speed, but requires a relatively smaller force to maintain that speed. In swimming it means that it is much simpler for a swimmer to maintain a steady swimming speed, by a constant application of force, rather than having an uneven, broken type of movement with changes in pace which would require considerable additional effort and energy expenditure. To some extent, this is why the alternating strokes, such as Front Crawl and Back Crawl are faster and easier than the simultaneous strokes, such as Breaststroke and Butterfly.

Transfer of momentum

An example of transfer of momentum is when a moving ball hits a stationary one. Sometimes the second ball will move away leaving the first one standing still, i.e., the momentum from the first ball has been transferred to the second. In swimming, a good example of this might be in a racing dive, particularly the "wind up" start. The strong, vigorous, circular motion of the arms is used to develop a powerful movement which, when the arms are stopped at the correct moment, is transferred to the momentum of the body as it leaves the starting block. An example of poor transfer of momentum would be when a swimmer's arm actions are uneven or hesitant, which then results in energy wasting jerky or bobbing body movements.

Chapter 9

Observation and Stroke Analysis – Mechanics as applied to the strokes

Lynn Hogarth

Introduction

Observation may be defined as accurate watching and the collection and recording of facts. These are the first key points in Stroke Analysis – to look at carefully, to collect and record facts.

Analysis is the process of dividing an object or action into component parts or elements and the minute examination of each part. This is precisely the process followed when analysing a stroke. Stroke analysis, therefore, can be defined as the dividing of a stroke into component parts, and the examining of each part carefully in order to collect the facts and record them. There is no great mystique involved in stroke analysis once the methods of breaking down a stroke and looking at what happens above and below the water level are mastered.

Approach

The teacher/coach must find a simple method of approach. Once the stroke analysis is complete the teacher/coach should be able to "picture" swimmers without being able to physically observe them. The analysis should also enable any other person with basic stroke knowledge to read it and also picture that swimmer's stroke. The comments and the words used should relate accurately to the stroke patterns observed.

Text Book versus Individual Style

It is important to remember that every individual swims with their own style. The aim of a good teacher/coach is to convey to the swimmer a stroke which is as near to the text book, i.e., mechanically efficient, as is possible within the constraints of the individual's capabilities, strength, etc. Teachers/coaches should be clear in their knowledge of the text book stroke, before observing their swimmers' techniques.

Basic Analysis Format

As the skill of stroke analysis has developed the format used has become known as 'B.L.A.B.T.' This phrase represents the initials of the component parts common to all strokes:

B – Body Position

L – Leg Action

A – Arm Action

B – Breathing

T – Timing (Also known as Co-ordination)

BLABT gives a logical sequence to follow when analysing a stroke. The addition of a first impression and a final assessment completes the picture. Stroke analysis becomes, therefore:

OBSERVE – First Impression
ANALYSE – Examine Component Parts of Stroke (BLABT)
ASSESS – Final Picture

The following the major areas should be covered when doing a stroke analysis:

First Impression (Observation)

Stroke Efficiency – is the swimmer moving through the water with ease and the minimum amount of effort?

Streamlining – is the swimmer displaying a streamlined position?

Continuity and timing – is the swimmer showing a continuous arm and leg action and does the timing look correct?

BLABT (Analysis)

In the same manner that the stroke is divided into component parts in order to observe it, the parts are sub-divided and viewed in a logical sequence.

Body position

Head
● position in relation to water level
● position in relation to the rest of the body
● type and amount of movement when swimming

Shoulders
● position in relation to the water level
● position in relation to the rest of the body
● type and amount of movement when swimming

Hips
● position in relation to water level
● position in relation to the rest of the body
● type and amount of movement when swimming

Legs
● position in relation to water level
● position in relation to rest of the body, in particular the hips

Leg action

Propulsion
● does the leg action aid propulsion?
● is the leg action the main or the secondary source of propulsion?

Balance
● does the leg action balance the stroke?

Depth
- in relation to the range of the swimmer's body

  N.B. A deep kick on a tall swimmer is different from a deep kick on a short swimmer.

Rhythm
- is the kick continuous or interrupted?

Source
- from where does the kick originate?

Arm action

Entry of Hand – In strokes with overwater recovery
- position in relation to shoulder width
- position of hand on entry, e.g., palm out
- distance in relation to head position

Propulsive phase
- limb track – the path followed by the hand/arm throughout propulsion
- limb state – is the arm straight or bent in the main propulsive section?

Recovery
- hand/arm position as recovery begins
- hand/arm position during recovery, e.g., high elbow
- type of recovery – in or over water
- muscle state – tense or relaxed

Breathing
- inhalation in relation to stroke cycle
- exhalation in relation to stroke cycle
- position of inhalation, e.g., to the front
- type of breathing, e.g., explosive

Timing
- number of leg beats per arm cycle (Back Crawl, Front Crawl and Butterfly)
- relationship of arm action, leg action and breathing (Breaststroke)
- type of leg beats (Butterfly, e.g., major, minor)
- continuity of arm and leg action
- is there a catch up in the arm action? (Front Crawl and Back Crawl)

Final Picture (Assessment)

Having completed the observation and analysis by looking at both strengths and weaknesses in the swimmer's technique a final assessment can be made. The assessment will determine the technique to be recommended for that particular swimmer. There are many types of stroke analysis sheets. The one shown on page 81 follows the logical sequence used, giving sub-headings as a memory jogger for the teacher/coach. The needs of the four competitive strokes vary and the guidelines given in this chapter are intended as a basis for covering all of them.

STROKE ANALYSIS SHEET

Name of swimmer... Age.....................

Stroke to be analysed... Date...................

FIRST IMPRESSIONS
Stroke Efficiency
Streamlining
Continuity

BODY POSITION
Head
Shoulders
Hips
Legs

LEG ACTION
Propulsion
Balance
Depth
Rhythm

ARM ACTION
Entry
Propulsive Phase
Recovery

BREATHING
Position
Type

TIMING (Co-ordination)
Number of beats (Front Crawl, Back Crawl and Butterfly)
Type of beat (Butterfly)
Arm/leg action and breathing timing (Breaststroke)
Catch up (Alternating Strokes)

FINAL PICTURE

Contributory Factors

There are a number of other factors to be taken into account when making the final assessment and deciding on the technique to suit the individual swimmer:

Flexibility – the range of the swimmer's movements will have a bearing on the way a stroke is performed.

Age/strength – the age and strength of a swimmer may affect their ability to perform certain stroke movements.

Buoyancy – the natural buoyancy of a swimmer varies and can affect the body position, e.g., low floating position.

Tiredness – a swimmer's stroke will deteriorate when tired. This could result in an incorrect analysis of an individual's technique.

Analysis viewpoints

To get a true impression of the stroke it would be necessary to view it from in front, behind, the left and right sides, above and below. The conditions in most swimming pools would not usually allow vision from all angles, particularly from below; however, the stroke should be viewed from all possible angles. This may include from above by viewing from a balcony area or diving platform. An analysis made from one viewpoint could be quite inaccurate as the medium of water distorts the vision (refraction). The teacher/coach should alter his poolside position during analysis in order to gain as accurate a picture as possible.

Mechanics as applied to the strokes

Having considered the principles of stroke analysis it is now essential to relate them to the terminology of the mechanical principles introduced in Chapter 8. The main areas to be considered are the propulsive phases of all arm and leg actions in swimming. In three of the competitive strokes, Front Crawl, Back Crawl and Butterfly, the arm action provides the majority of the propulsion. In Breaststroke the leg action is still the main propulsive force although recent changes in technique have developed a stroke which provides more propulsion from the arm action than was previously possible.

Areas common to all strokes

Catch – this occurs in the early part of the arm action of all strokes. It is often thought to be the first movement in the arm action after the entry, but this is not always the case. A dictionary gives the meaning of the word "catch" as: "...to seize and hold".

For swimmers to move their bodies through the water they must use their arms as levers. A lever must have an anchor point (Catch Point). The hand must "seize" the water and try to keep "hold". The catch should come in the early part of the propulsive phase of the arm action, when the hands have been placed in the best position to obtain maximum leverage.

Because water is a liquid it is not possible to seize and hold in the same way that a solid can be held. A slipping effect is felt. The hand must continually adjust and find still water, e.g., as seen in a sculling movement. The swimmer who can obtain an early catch with a minimal amount of slipping will be able to propel their body further with each stroke. The position of the catch in each stroke will be detailed later in this chapter.

Propulsive Phase

The manner in which a propulsive phase is described has gradually changed over the years due to new information about underwater stroke patterns with the hands and arms. As already explained in Chapter 8, better observation of underwater stroke technique, and consequent experiments, have revealed that good propulsion is achieved when limbs use curved or elliptical pathways, i.e., move into still water.

The terminology of pulling and pushing is, perhaps, now less appropriate. The word sweep has been adopted and is now often used when describing the arm action of all four competitive strokes and also the leg action of Breaststroke. (Refer back to Fig. 8.8).

"Sweeps and Beats"

As in everything concerned with human movement swimming is multi-dimensional, and so the propulsive sweeps have to be considered in the same manner. After studying all underwater stroke patterns four basic arm actions have been identified:

- outsweep
- insweep
- downsweep
- upsweep

The leg actions in the Front Crawl, Back Crawl and Butterfly strokes display an up and down action which can easily be expressed as beats, i.e., upbeat and downbeat. The prefix to the words sweep and beat describes clearly what is seen underwater, e.g., downsweep, upbeat.

The understanding of sweeps in stroke mechanics is not, in itself, the full answer to producing mechanically efficient strokes. Other factors have to be considered:

- **Pitch** – when a knife is sliced into and through butter using a sweeping action it slips through without gaining purchase (catch). In the same way, a hand slicing through water does not obtain a catch and, consequently, gains very little propulsion. In contrast, if a knife is placed in the butter sideways the sweeps would still be possible but there would be purchase (catch). The direction of inclination of the knife in the butter or the hand in swimming is referred to as the **pitch,** and it is important that the hand be pitched correctly on entry, at catch and throughout the propulsive phase of all strokes.

Figure 9.1 Angle of attack.

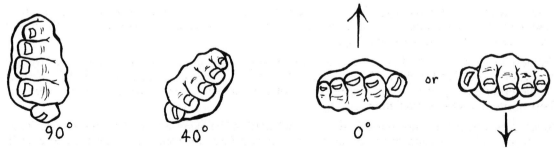

- **Angle of Attack** – what is the correct pitch? The degree of pitch of the hand or foot throughout a stroke is referred to as the **Angle of Attack.** The angle of attack varies at different points within the

83

propulsive phase and the exact angle is very difficult to observe without underwater shots of a swimmer. Angles of between 20° and 50° seem the most **effective,** with angles of 0° (flat) and 90° (vertical) being the most ineffective.

● **Limb Speed** – the other factor which affects propulsion and the amount of movement in a forward direction is limb speed. Water is a fluid which moves when pressure is applied to it. When swimmers catch the water they apply pressure to it, this pressure causes the water to move and the only way swimmers can continue to apply pressure is by increasing the speed of the limb movement throughout the propulsive phase. This applies to all stroke patterns.

Identifying the elements of stroke mechanics

How does a teacher/coach set about identifying all the elements detailed? Knowledge can be gained by watching world class swimmers in action on film or video. Special attention should be paid to underwater shots. The points to be viewed are:

● catch point in each stroke
● direction of sweeps during propulsion
● direction pitch
● angle of attack
● limb speed

Most world class swimmers use propulsive actions that relate closely to the 'Text Book Stroke', and the actions observed will give the teacher/coach good guidelines to follow.

Conveying stroke mechanics to the swimmer

Some swimmers will display the correct stroke mechanics without apparently having to be taught the stroke patterns. These swimmers have a natural 'feel' for the water. Feel is a swimmer's ability to search out the correct movements, the intrinsic feedback to which reference was made in Chapter 2, and handle the water effectively. It is the element that is often referred to as 'natural talent'. Chapter 2 described how this "feel" could be taught or coached with the aid of teacher/coach feedback (extrinsic) on the correctness of the movements and positions. Regular practice of these movements, with teacher/coach feedback, is particularly important in a swimmer's developmental years. Skills should, however, be continually practised throughout a swimmers' career to allow for the changes which occur as each swimmer develops as an individual.

Major faults in stroke mechanics

Most of the areas covered in this chapter are common to all strokes. A swimmer displaying a fault in the mechanics of one stroke may also display the same fault in another stroke. Faults in stroke mechanics will always result in reduced propulsion and may also result in poor body position. Faults are often due to a lack of understanding of the mechanics and, once rectified in one stroke, will also often be rectified in all strokes.

● **dropped elbow** – as described in Chapter 8, the arms work as levers with the hand working as a paddle. For the hand to be an effective paddle it must control the stroke. If the elbow does not remain high during Front Crawl, Butterfly and Breaststroke the hand is unable to control the stroke and carry out the necessary sweeps which produce maximum propulsion. When a swimmer drops the elbow it leads the stroke and, therefore, the swimmer is unable to carry out the correct sweeps, pitch and angle of attack. In Back Crawl, however, during the propulsive phase, the elbow is low.

- **incorrect angle of attack** – the correct angle is dependent on the phase of the arm action and also the type of stroke being performed. As already stated an angle of 0° or 90° can be considered incorrect. A palm down angle of attack (0°) at the beginning of the propulsive phase would lift the upper body upwards, increasing resistance and reducing streamlining. This would occur in all strokes. Similarly a palm up angle of attack (0°) at the completion of the Front Crawl, Back Crawl and Butterfly propulsive phases would push the body downwards and reduce streamlining. A slicing angle of attack (90°) in the early part of a stroke, would result in a swimmer not obtaining a catch and would consequently, little propulsion would be achieved.

Summary

- in stroke analysis it is important to **observe, analyse** and **assess** in a logical sequence throughout the stroke in order to obtain a true picture of the swimmer
- all **contributory factors** should be taken into account before deciding on a stroke to suit the swimmer being analysed
- analysis should be viewed from **all angles possible** in order to obtain a complete picture
- mechanics should be considered in relation to curved or elliptical pathways
- **the terminology used should relate to the above**
- all elements should be **identified** and **analysed**
- the basic principles of stroke mechanics should be given as feed back to assist the swimmer in the development of sound technique.

PART IV

THE APPLICATION OF THE PRINCIPLES IN PRACTICE

Introduction to Part IV

Part IV of this book is designed to increase the readers' knowledge of the skills and techniques of swimming. That knowledge should be related to the theoretical aspects of learning and teaching/coaching outlined in Parts I-III. In particular, the chapters on the strokes are written on the assumption that very careful attention will have been given to Chapter 9, **Observation and Stroke Analysis, mechanics as applied to the strokes,** which suggests a structured approach to developing stroke technique.

The major elements of Part IV are dealt with under the headings of non-swimmer and beginner activities, the four main strokes and an introduction to diving. However, there is also an "End Piece" outlining some other general swimming activities not covered elsewhere in the book. The stroke chapters make no reference to ASA laws. This is deliberate, and readers are reminded that these laws change from time to time. If teachers/coaches are involved in competition swimming the current laws should always be consulted for the most up-to-date rulings. Failure to make this precautionary check could seriously disadvantage their swimmers.

Chapter 10

Teaching the non-swimmer and beginner

Anne Cradock

Introduction

If the needs of the non-swimmer and beginner can be properly identified then the possibilities of providing a comfortable, safe and stimulating learning environment can be greatly increased.

Comfort

Temperature – pupils are more relaxed if the air temperature in the changing room and pool surround is warm and slightly higher than the water temperature which should also be comfortably warm, say 27°C (80°F).

Length of lesson – early lessons, especially with younger children, should be short, active and enjoyable. Where the water temperature is less than ideal, the lesson should be shortened and activities chosen should be lively with the pupils' shoulders in the water.

Quiet and friendly – a quiet, friendly environment is more welcoming to young or uncertain beginners.

Parents and babies – babies are happiest with a parent close by and eye contact maintained. Babies are often held in a 'cuddle' position as they enter the water and this may also be maintained until the baby relaxes in the water. The water temperature here ideally needs to be between 28°-30°C (82°-86°F).

Young children – quickly adjust to this new and exciting environment if they are surrounded by brightly coloured inviting toys and, sometimes, familiar music.

Adults – feel more comfortable in a class and pool on their own alongside other adults learning to swim. Onlookers should be kept to the minimum wherever possible.

Knowledge of the environment

Changing – learners are more confident if they are familiar with the procedure of attending the swimming pool and know where the changing room, toilet and shower facilities are located. They need to know where and how their clothes are stored and whether they need a coin or a token for a locker.

Pool – in the pool they should know where to go for their lesson, where the learner pool or shallow end is and the rope or sign indicating the limit of shallow water.

Reassurance – pupils need to feel safe, and it will be helpful if a shallow learner pool is available exclusively for the use of the non-swimmer class.

Roped area – a rope should mark the limit of shallow water.

Partner spotter system – older pupils and adults are reassured by the knowledge that a partner is keeping an eye on them and vice versa.

Swimming aids – availability, suitability and desirability

Support – a swimming aid can provide the necessary physical or psychological support needed at this stage to enable the learner to explore the water with greater confidence.

Type of aid – the type of aid chosen depends on the preference, age and size of pupil, the amount of support required or desired and the preference of the teacher.

Position in the water – it is important that the aid chosen allows the pupil to float **in** the water, to have freedom of arm movement and buoyancy that can be progressively reduced.

Fitting and inflation – pupils should be supervised when aids are being fitted to check that the correct size is selected and that the aid is properly fitted and suitably inflated with stoppers replaced.

Time without aid – some time during each lesson should be spent without the aid.

The use of the various swimming aids is discussed in detail in Chapter 4.

Confidence

Relationship – a good teacher-pupil relationship is essential in this situation where pupils are most vulnerable. Pupils place their trust in their teachers and they must respect and have confidence in them.

Teacher-pupil ratio – it is helpful if the teacher-pupil ratio is high and the non-swimmer/beginner class numbers are low, say, a maximum of 10 or 12 but, preferably, as low as 6. Success and progress are closely linked to small class sizes at this level.

Team teaching – progress can be improved if other qualified assistants are available to assist in the water whilst the class-teacher remains on the side. This is particularly helpful in the case of a very timid pupil.

Block teaching – success in learning to swim is increased in the early stages where lessons are frequent and shorter, with short intervals between each lesson, e.g., 10 shorter lessons in two weeks rather than 10 longer lessons in a school term.

Exploration

To help pupils to adapt, and learn to love water, there should be opportunities for freedom and exploration without fear or failure or embarrassment.

Play – opportunity to 'play' in the water is as important for learner adults as for young children. Enjoyment is a key factor in motivation to learn.

Age appropriate – the activities and language should be appropriate to the age of the pupils.

Music – music enjoyed by the pupils can be used in the beginner lesson and can be relaxing or stimulating and can be a beneficial aid to teaching.

Knowledge and understanding

Taught skills – the teacher progressively introduces essential skills. Some of our knowledge comes from 'finding out' and some comes from understanding what we have been taught. It is important that we know what to do, how to do it and why we are doing it.

Understanding – it is important that pupils (or parents in the case of babies or toddlers) understand what they are doing and why. Adult learners find this an essential part of the learning process.

Practice – opportunities to attempt the skills learned to reinforce the knowledge and perfect the skill are important.

Success – tasks set must be attainable and accessible to all at their own learning and skill level.

Individual tasks – pupils respond well to individual tasks related to the general task.

Whole-part-whole – it is important to allow the pupil to attempt the WHOLE skill or stroke enabling the teacher to decide the PART of the skill or stroke which needs practice. See Chapters 2 and 3 for more on the Whole-Part-Whole method.

Recording – a major motivating factor for all learners is to record and measure their progress.
Challenge – tasks must be progressive, relevant and challenging.
Fun – moving in the water is fun; learning is fun; if it is fun for the teacher it is fun for the pupil.

Teaching methods and approaches

Shallow water method – this is a method by which pupils achieve a horizontal position in the water with their hands on the pool floor. An appropriate depth is such that the chin is on the water while the hands are on the pool floor with arms extended (30-45 cms (12″-18″) for younger pupils). This method used to be limited to learner pools or the broad horizontal steps leading to these pools. The advent of leisure pools with "beaches" has increased the opportunity for using this method, provided that the wave machine is not operating! The shallow water method can be used with or without swimming aids and has the advantage of the pupils' faces being out of the water.

Prone (front downwards) – the pupils move forward by sliding their hands along the floor of the pool, progressing to making stepping movements with the hands. The legs float behind in an extended position. Eventually the arms pull the body forward without making contact with the floor. The pupils can then be encouraged to add a gentle kick.

Supine (face upwards) – from a sitting position, pupils can be encouraged to lie back putting their heads on the pillow of the water. The pupils' hands are flat on the pool floor with fingers pointing towards their feet. The progressions are as for the prone position.

The advantage of the shallow water method is that pupils can easily stop by either kneeling or sitting.

Figure 10.1
Shallow water method – prone position.

Figure 10.2
Shallow water method – supine position.

Deep water method

With this method pupils wear inflated, close fitting swimming aids and could possibly swim out of their depth. Babies and toddlers have always learned by this method because they are always out of their depth, even in shallow learner pools.

Safety – it must be noted, however, that the pupils mentioned above have adult support in the water, if necessary, and that the same conditions should be available if this is to apply to other beginner classes.

The advantages of the deep water method are:

● pupils are experiencing the upthrust of the water throughout the lesson.
● pupils breathe regularly while they are moving and tire less quickly.
● pupils return to shallow water for the removal of swimming aids and for submersion activities.

Partner support

This method should be used only occasionally and with classes which are able to respond in a confident and responsible manner in a supporting role.

Adults – respond very well to working with a partner and learn from helping each other. Partner work often gives them a much needed rest as well as a chance to chat and share experiences with a fellow learner.

Children – can respond very positively when given this responsibility. This method can be useful if equipment is limited.

Limitations – when pupils are supporting or assisting a partner they are not actually practising. Water time is so valuable that it is essential to aim for maximum activity for all pupils.

Flipper float method

This method requires a 1:1 teacher-pupil ratio and is suitable for a timid pupil when there is no adult to support in the water and where nothing else has worked.

Teacher – standing on the poolside holding a pole with a rope supporting a rubber cover loop which is under the armpits of the swimmer.

The pupil – holds one float with two hands, arms are fully extended, chin on the water. With flippers on its feet the pupil kicks its legs gently up and down whilst the teacher walks alongside. The amount of support is gradually reduced and as the pupil develops confidence and swims out of the hoop. The same process can be repeated if necessary in a supine position. The float should either be held about half way along its length, with thumbs on top and fingers underneath, or with the forearms resting along the top of the float. (Fig. 10.3).

Figure 10.3 Float holding.

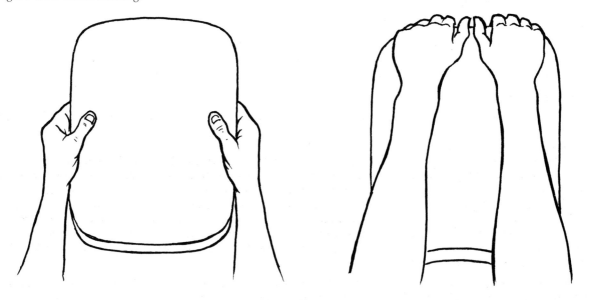

Multi-stroke method

This method involves the strokes being introduced alongside each other with an equal emphasis on the basic technique for each stroke. The leg actions of the crawl strokes are combined with an arm action with an underwater arm recovery and the circular Breaststroke leg kick is combined with an arm action with a circular pathway. Pupils usually find the type of action and position in the water of one of the strokes is more natural to them. The chosen stroke then receives greater emphasis in the following lessons but with some time still being spent on progressively improving the other strokes.

Very young children

These children often find the alternating crawl strokes more natural. Initially they may move around in a very upright position, preferring to be on their front, if they like to see where they are going, or on their back, when they have less difficulty with water splashing in their faces.

Adults

Adult learners like to both see where they are going and be able to chat with their friends (and, sometimes, keep their hair dry!). Such sessions are often very sociable. The Breaststroke arm action is often preferred by adults as being very supportive.

Some adults are afraid of the water and it is important for the teacher/coach to try and find out both why this is and what is motivating them to learn at this particular point in their lives. Part of the fear element is often related to the possibility of making a fool of themselves in public; therefore, the fewer the spectators the better. Other factors which might influence the adult learner might be:

- that physical difficulties, perhaps related to joint mobility and muscle use in general, make exercise something to be approached with caution
- that they are perhaps easily fatigued
- that they will have a high level of motivation
- that they are capable of longer attention spans than children
- the need to know why they are doing something
- that they are often ready to provide mutual self-help in a very responsible manner.

The timid pupil

The teacher/coach must find an approach which enables the timid pupil to join in without losing face, and it is helpful if the learning environment described earlier can be maintained.

Stroke hybrids – at this early stage of learning, following a period of exploration and experimentation where pupils find out the effects that pulling, pushing, sculling and kicking have on changing their position, direction or movement through the water, it may be that the choice and combination of arm and leg action does not produce a recognised stroke. These strokes are called stroke hybrids and provide fun alternatives as well as challenging co-ordination exercises. Clearly the main strokes, as we know them, are the most efficient methods of travelling through the water. However, at this early stage pupils should be free to develop their own method of moving through the water or combine, say, a simultaneous arm action with an alternating leg kick and vice versa – prone, supine or on their side. Movement can be head or feet first through or under the water surface.

Overwater recovery arm actions tend to be introduced at a later stage when the leg kick is strong enough to keep the body relatively flat while the arms come out of the water.

Equipment for teaching non-swimmers and beginners

The question of types and use of swimming aids is fully dealt with in Chapter 4, but some points concerning their use for non-swimmers and beginners in particular are offered here:

- it is helpful to have a variety of both size and type of swimming aid to enable both pupil and teacher to choose those which will give the required physical or psychological support.
- the age and size of the pupils, as well as the size of the class, will determine range and nature of the swimming aids required.

Objects which float, and which can be blown or pushed along using parts of the head, arm, leg, etc., e.g., boats, fishes, frogs, are very popular with younger children, whilst adults and older children might prefer footballs, beachballs, etc. Hoops are also useful because they can be held at a variety of levels, float on the water surface, or just under in a vertical position or rest on the pool floor.

Objects and toys which sink are also useful for developing underwater confidence, e.g., plastic pegs, Airflow balls, coffee jar lids painted with colours or numbers, weighted rings, sticks, heavy plastic flowers. Other items which encourage breathing out or blowing along are table tennis balls, "poached eggs" (similar to a table tennis ball inside a disc), and small inflatable toys. Things often used to encourage young children to have fun by pouring, sprinkling, squirting are small plastic buckets, watering cans, washing-up liquid bottles, water pistols. In addition the teacher/coach might find such things as traffic light coloured circles for games, plastic bands for 'tails', percussion instruments, e.g., drum, bells, shaker, chime bar, useful for movement orientation activities.

The skills – why and how?

To enable pupils to become confident and competent in the water they need to be taught and to discover the following essential skills:

Entry into the water
- with or without assistance
- backwards down the steps (Fig. 10.4)
- from a sitting position twist hands across the body, palms flat on poolside, rotate body and lower (Fig. 10.5)
- from a standing position, drop or jump in, depending on the water depth, to a partner or without a partner.

Movement – done in a standing position with shoulders under the water to feel the effect of water pressure and resistance (with or without swimming aids):
- walking, sliding feet, with a wide base for balance, arms spread just under the surface in front of the body, moving forwards, backwards, sideways or with a turn
- arms begin to pull, push and scull, alternating or simultaneously
- following a variety of pathways, walking following the shape of a circle, triangle, square, figure of eight; increasing or decreasing the size of the shape, linking the shapes together, letter-shapes, writing their own name
- varying the speed of movement through the water, slowly, quickly and finding out how changes of speed occur and the effect the changes have on them in the water.

Figure 10.4 Entry into the water from steps.

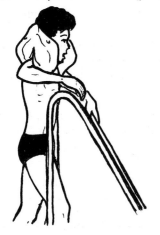

Figure 10.5 Entry into the water from sitting position.

Methods of getting feet off the bottom

These practices can be performed with, then without, swimming aids as appropriate to the non-swimmer or beginner.

Vertical position

- marching on the spot, lifting knees high, chin on the water, arms spread and pressing down, feet gradually not touching the pool floor on the downward movements
- head up, knees tucked, turning on the spot. Pressing against the water with the arms helps the turning.

Holding the rail
- undergrasp, forearms against the wall (Fig. 10.6).
- one hand overgrasp, the other hand **directly** underneath – palm facing wall, fingers pointing down (Fig. 10.7).
- overgrasp at rail, or over the edge of the pool in deck level pools, forearms down the wall, elbows pressing against the wall (Fig. 10.8).

Figure 10.6 Holding rail – undergrasp.

Figure 10.7 Holding side – hands spread vertically.

Figure 10.8 Holding side – deck level pools.

Regaining the feet from the prone position

It is important, at this stage, that pupils practise the skill of regaining their feet to enable them to regain balance and stop **before** they are required to push and glide or move in a horizontal position. Most young pupils will naturally perform the correct movements but others, and older beginners, find it useful to know exactly what they are doing and why. They can then be their own teacher, repeating the teaching points for themselves or a partner.

From the prone position at the rail (as above) the pupil will be able to press down against the rail to initiate the head lift. However, the full regaining the feet from the prone position is described below (Fig. 10.9):

Action	Teaching point
● press down and back with both arms	● 'press'
● lift the head	● 'head up' – legs start to sink
● bend the knees	● 'knees up' – knees move forward
● press or plant the feet to the floor	● 'stand up'

If further practices are necessary, pupils could try:
- facing the rail without holding, arms straight palms facing down
- facing partner resting palms on partner's upturned palms
- holding two floats, holding one float then, later, without float support

Figure 10.9 Regaining the feet from the prone position.

Push and glide in the prone position

This is another essential early skill; it provides initial momentum enabling the pupil to achieve a horizontal position and is a good method of starting off. Activities could include:

- push and glide from pool floor to the poolside
- push and glide away from the wall to a partner
- push and glide away from the wall and regain feet on own
- back towards the wall, both hands on the rail, legs bent, feet high on the wall, head down and push way from wall

Figure 10.10 Push and glide in the prone position.

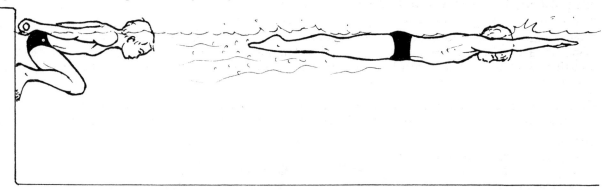

Regaining the feet from the supine position

It may be helpful initially to have a partner standing behind to assist the forward movement.

Action
- allow arms to sink, press down and back

Teaching point
- 'head up', head moves forward and up

97

- turn palms to facing feet and push towards feet and tuck knees
- press or plant feet to the floor

- 'knees up', leaning forwards

- 'stand up'

This skill can initially be practised between two floats; then it could be tried whilst wearing armbands with a partner standing behind. Later it could be done with the partner standing beside the pupil's feet encouraging a reaching forward action. The partner should first be taught how to help before being asked to assist.

Figure 10.11 Regaining the feet from the supine position.

Push and glide in the supine position

Once pupils have mastered the skill of regaining their feet from a supine horizontal floating position, they can try the supine push and glide:

- from pool floor gently backwards towards the rail
- from facing the rail, backwards towards a partner and regain feet
- from facing the rail, backwards and regain feet unaided

Propulsion

The initial aim is to enable pupils to propel themselves on their fronts, backs and sides, both on and, eventually, under the surface, and to be able to change direction, bodyshape and to use alternating and simultaneous arm and leg actions.

Exploration of leg actions – using two floats, and with the previous practice of both regaining feet prone and supine and pushing and gliding, pupils can easily attempt an alternating kick on their front and back, changing from one to the other by lifting their heads, tucking their legs and allowing them to drop and swing through into the other position in the water:

- the above method can be used with the alternating crawl type kick, the Breaststroke kick and the Butterfly leg kick
- pupils can easily change position in this way in the water using one float held in two hands once they are confident

Figure 10.12 Exploration of body positions and leg actions.

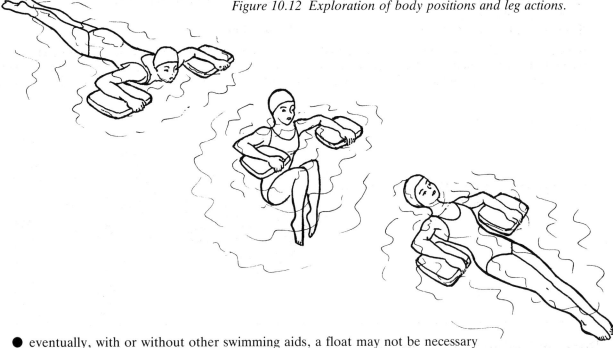

- eventually, with or without other swimming aids, a float may not be necessary
- pupils should also explore leg kicks which they can achieve while lying on their side. Often the Breaststroke leg kick can be more easily learned in a vertical position using two floats.

Figure 10.13 Breaststroke leg kick in the vertical position using two floats.

Exploration of arm actions – at this stage all recovery movements are under water. Pulling or pushing actions towards the feet will produce head first travel in either prone or supine position. Later, let them explore pulling, sculling and pushing movements with one arm at a time or both arms, to discover how movement head first, feet first, prone or supine, and sideways and turning movements can be achieved.

Rotation and orientation

- prone push and glide then longitudinal roll over to look at the ceiling
- prone push and glide, lift head, tuck knees put ears in the water and stretch out on to the back. The movement is similar to that shown in Fig. 10.12, but without the floats
- supine push and glide, roll over to continue on the front
- supine push and glide, lift head, tuck legs, and stretch out on the front (Fig. 10.14)
- pupils can then rotate from one stroke into another – carrying on in the same direction by rotating around the longitudinal axis and changing direction by rotating around the lateral axis.

Figure 10.14 Orientation.

Submersion

To be able to submerge, regain the surface in a variety of ways with different body parts making contact with the pool floor are all useful practices.

Face in the water and breath control – before pupils are asked to explore under the water surface they need to be able to hold their breath. The teacher can count seconds and the pupils can see how long they can hold their breath with their faces out of the water initially, they can then try with their faces in the water. The pupils can also try pushing a ball/float along the water surface with their chin, their nose, then their forehead – progressively lowering their face into the water without thinking about it.

Eyes open under water – counting objects on the pool floor; collecting different coloured objects or ones with particular markings on them; partner games with fists open/closed, one open one closed, etc.

Regaining the surface – through pressing feet down and standing up. Also teach pressing down with the hands and arms, then raising head or hands to the surface.

Early submerging practice – holding the side of pool/partner's hands, kneel, sit on the pool floor and then, touch pool floor with other body parts, e.g., tummy, back, elbow, shoulder, etc.

Push and glide to submerge – feet high on wall, head down, push down to the pool floor, straight arms, hands leading, keeping chin on chest.

Re-surface from underwater, push and glide – tuck knees, lift head, place feet on the pool floor and stand up or swim up or raise head, point hands to surface and glide up to the surface.

Under and through games – using hoops, partner's arm, partner's legs astride to go under and through. There are also games in and out of hoops which are floating freely on the water surface, e.g., duck under and into, dive out of.

Breathing

Following the breath-holding skills tried earlier while their faces were in the water, pupils can be encouraged to breathe regularly while moving through the water both in walking and swimming positions. This can be most easily achieved by some of the following methods:

Very young children – singing games and nursery rhymes in the water.

Adults – encouraging them to 'chat' to each other while they are moving. By doing this they will be breathing at the same time.

Exhalation – blowing out (exhalation) vigorously is important before breathing in (inhalation) can take place. This can be encouraged initially by challenging them to blow bubbles at the surface, or to blow small floatable objects, e.g., table tennis balls, along the surface. Beginners should be gently encouraged to exhale with their face in the water as soon as they are confident to do so. Very young children can try this skill in the bath – preferably, before the soap is put in!

Once the pupils have learned how to exhale into the water, they then need to learn to breathe in relation to the arm action of the prone strokes. Just when to do it, and how to move the head to enable the mouth to break the surface to enable inhalation will be found in later chapters.

Floatation

It is important to help pupils become aware of where their body is, the shape it is making and how this affects their balance in the water. Apart from previously described "narrow" shapes in the push and glide prone and supine positions, there are also "star" shapes (prone and supine), and tucked shapes in various positions, one of the most well known being the "mushroom" float (Fig. 10.15) which involves fully inflated lungs and a tight tucked shape of the body.

Figure 10.15 Mushroom float.

Exit

Pupils should be encouraged to use a variety of methods of leaving the pool, e.g., using the steps initially, then up and over the side. To climb over the side, the hands are placed on the top of the wall and the swimmer jumps or kicks hard downwards. If out of the depth then the kick raises the body out of the water, the arms are straightened by pressing vigorously downwards and a knee or foot is placed on the poolside.

The Front and Back Paddles

Depending on the progress of the individual within any group the time will arrive for introducing the basic actions for the front (prone) and back (supine) swimming positions. Usually the movements take the form of the Front Paddle (formerly called the "Doggie" Paddle) and Back Paddle.

Front Paddle (Fig. 10.16) – the swimmer is in a prone and horizontal position. The leg action is similar to that of Front Crawl. The alternating arm action, however, takes place totally underwater by pulling downwards and backwards from a forward position, and then recovering by stretching the hands forward from close to the chest to a point in advance of the shoulders. Initially, the swimmer will probably make short arm movements, but as confidence grows these actions become longer and more powerful.

Back Paddle and Sculling (Fig. 10.17) – the swimmer is supine and close to the horizontal position. The leg action is similar to that of Back Crawl. In the early stages the arm movements usually consist of simultaneous sweeping actions towards the feet. Whilst this action produces considerable power the recovery also creates a great deal of resistance. Gradually, the swimmer should be encouraged to keep the arms closer to the thighs so that the movements become the familiar circling or "figure of eight" sculling action. As the hands move away from the body the leading edges (little fingers) are raised so that the palms are facing outwards and downwards. The leading edges (thumbs) on the inward movement are again raised so that the palms face inwards and downwards. At the outer and innermost points in the action the wrists rotate to change the pitch of the palms. The arms remain fairly straight and without undue tension. The tilting (pitch) of the palms at different angles influences whether the swimmer remains stationary or travels in a head first or feet first direction.

Figure 10.16 Front paddle.

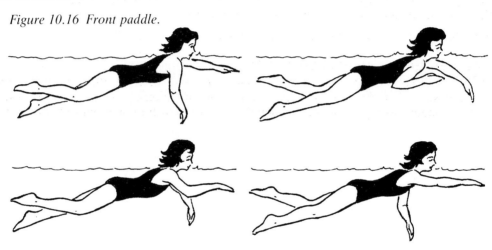

Figure 10.17 Back paddle.

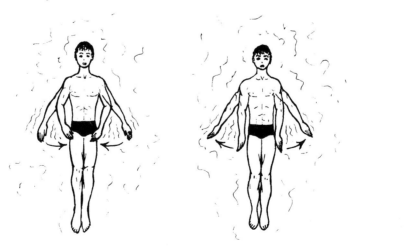

The content of the non-swimmer and beginner lesson

This lesson should be exciting, challenging and reassuring to the pupils new to the class. There should be:

- safe confident entry (see entry skills on page 94)
- good organisation and supervision to ensure that each pupil has enough space and time to enter independently
- a lively, exciting warm up activity or game encouraging independent movement, vertical or horizontal
- teaching at a level relevant to the individual pupil
- an occasional testing of the skills, e.g., using the appropriate ASA Award Scheme
- a concluding game encouraging the basic practice of some of the previous skills
- short time for the practice of skill of the learner's own choice.

More detailed reference to lesson planning will be found in Chapters 1 and 3.

Further information for specialised groups

Parents and babies, parents and toddlers, adults and non-swimmers with disabilities all require very careful consideration to ensure that the environment, equipment and methods employed are relevant and appropriate. Other publications providing more details of how to teach these groups will be found in Part V of this book.

Chapter 11

Front Crawl

Nick Sellwood

Introduction

The fluency, power and low level of resistance makes Front Crawl the fastest swimming stroke yet developed. Unlike the other strokes, however, it does not have a specific competitive event, and is swum completely under Freestyle. Because of its efficiency the stroke is utilised over a range of distances up to 1500 metres, and is used in more competitive swimming events than any other stroke. Little wonder, therefore, that the world famous multiple Olympic medallists have been extremely good Front Crawl swimmers. Mark Spitz and Matt Biondi won the majority of their gold medals in freestyle events.

The Front Crawl stroke is continuing to evolve with slight differences in style being seen with respect to the needs of the event, i.e., distance Front Crawl swimmers tend to use a 2 beat leg kick for the majority of the race, whereas 50 metre sprinters tend to use a faster leg kick.

General description of the stroke

The swimmer is in a streamlined, prone position. Arm and leg actions are alternating and continuous. The arms recover over the water with legs kicking in a mostly vertical plane. The body rolls about its longitudinal axis with the head turning to the side to breathe. The hands trace a series of sculling type actions and accelerate in the water as they sweep downwards, inwards and finally upwards in the water.

Details of the stroke

Body position

The body should be in a prone, streamlined and almost horizontal position. The head, shoulders, hips and feet should be on or close to the surface. The body position does not remain static, but rolls about 45 degrees around the longitudinal axis. At the end of the body roll the head turns to breathe. The head does not deviate from the mid-line position when the breath is taken.

Leg action

Upbeat

The leg is extended and straight with the foot in a stretched (plantarflexed) position. The thigh initiates the rise of the leg and the knee flexes slightly, allowing the foot to rise in preparation for the downbeat. The basic movement of the leg is in the vertical plane, although some lateral kicking might result from the rotation of the body about its longitudinal axis.

Downbeat

This is initiated from the hips. Once the upper leg has moved 20-25cms (8-10 inches), the foot starts to whip downwards until the leg is fully extended. The foot is in a plantarflexed position and inwardly angled (in-toed).

Timing of leg kick

There are essentially 3 different timing patterns in Front Crawl; the 2 beat, 4 beat and 6 beat leg actions. The two beat pattern consists of one leg kick per arm stroke, whilst the six beat leg pattern is the most popular and consists of one downbeat per sweep on each arm stroke thus giving a total of six leg beats to a complete cycle of the arms. The four beat kick has two different varieties, although basically it is a combination of the previous two methods. The first of the 4 beat kicks is identified by a classic 6 beat pattern being executed by one leg whilst the other leg utilises a two beat timing. The second variation is a form based upon the 6 beat pattern with a pausing of the legs upon upsweep of each arm stroke.

Variations on leg kick

The legs may be seen to produce a cross-over type action in response to the individual breathing. This is a reaction by the leg kick to counteract the body roll, thus ensuring that the body maintains a streamlined position.

Arm action

Entry

Upon entry the arm is slightly flexed at the elbow and the hand slides into the water initially with the thumb and first finger with the palm facing outwards and angled at approximately 35 degrees. The entry position is in front of the head mid-way between the shoulder and the head. Once the hand has entered the water the wrist and elbow follow with the elbow remaining high.

Downsweep

From the entry position the hand moves forwards, still remaining close to the surface of the water. When the arm nears full extension the hand sculls outwards and 'catches' the water. From this position the hand sweeps downwards with the elbow beginning to flex, thus ensuring that the hand keeps travelling in a downward direction. The elbow is kept high throughout the downsweep as the hand starts to accelerate.

Insweep

As the downsweep nears completion the elbow begins to increase in flexion and the pitch of the hand turns inwards. This flexion continues throughout the insweep until it reaches 90 degrees. The acceleration of the hand continues to increase throughout this phase.

Upsweep

The upsweep is the final underwater phase of arm pull. From the insweep the hand pitch adjusts again to a backward and outward position. The fingers remain pointing at the bottom of the pool, until the final stages of the upsweep. When the hand passes the hips the wrist rotates, the palm turns inwards and releases the water. This places the little finger close to the surface in preparation for exit and recovery. The arm at this point is close to full extension.

Recovery

The elbow leads the recovery phase and is followed by the hand leaving the water, the little finger first. The arm travels forwards close to the head in a relaxed position. The elbow remains flexed and higher than the hand throughout the recovery. As the hand passes the shoulder the arm starts to extend forwards slightly in preparation for entry.

Figure 11.1 Full Front Crawl sequence – commencing at right hand entry. Shown from side view, head on and slightly below.

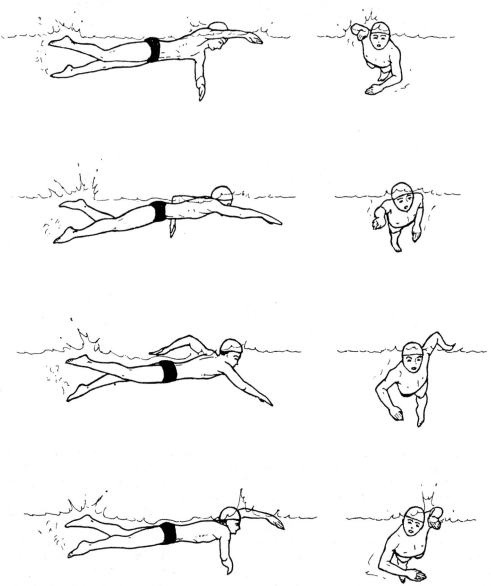

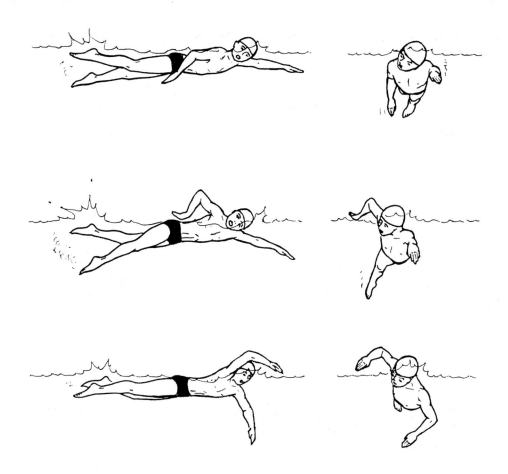

Breathing

Whilst the breath may be taken to either side of the body it should not disturb the rhythm of the stroke. The head turns in synchronisation with the natural body roll of the stroke. It is important to note that the head does not lift from the water. In terms of timing, the head rotates for breathing as the arm to the opposite side is entering the water and, once the breath is taken, returns to the central face down position. The forward momentum of the swimmer creates a bow wave behind which the breath is taken without lifting the head. Once the face is back in the water exhalation occurs in a controlled manner. The pattern of breaths to arm strokes varies from one breath to 2, 4 or 6 strokes (conventional unilateral breathing pattern), or a bilateral pattern of one breath to 3, 5, 7, etc., strokes. The type of breathing technique used also varies according to individuals whether utilising trickle breathing, where the air is exhaled gradually through the stroke cycle; or explosive breathing, where the swimmer turns the head to breathe in the air which is then expelled in a vigorous, short blast into the water.

Teaching/coaching points
Leg action
- **upbeat** – start the movement at the hips, the leg lifts upwards with the ankles and feet stretched
- **downbeat** – the movement starts at the hips and travels through the leg. The foot drives downwards until the leg is fully stretched

Arm action
- **entry** – arm enters the water in front of the shoulder with the palm facing outwards. Stretch the arm from its flexed position as the other arm completes the underwater phase
- **downsweep** – press hand outwards and sweep downwards and inwards with the palms turning throughout the movement
- **insweep** – hand continues to accelerate and the elbow bend increases
- **upsweep** – as the hand passes beneath the shoulder, accelerate upwards and backwards to the thigh
- **recovery** – lift the elbow in a relaxed style. Little finger follows and leaves water before the other fingers

Breathing
- turn the face sidewards as the body rolls to its maximum amount
- keep the head in the water
- return the face to the water as the body starts to roll back

Stroke practices/drills for Front Crawl

The greatest difficulty in learning Front Crawl is the mastery of breathing. It is strongly recommended that beginners should first concentrate on the arm and leg actions whilst holding the breath. Then, having established the techniques for breathing out into water as seperate practices, the co-ordination of the breathing action can be introduced into full stroke again, initially, over short distances. Whilst a wide range of examples of drills and practices are shown, teachers/coaches are encouraged to be selective and make use of them according to the needs of their swimmers.

Leg Action
- holding the rail, leg kick initiated from the hips (should only be done for brief periods)
- push off from the wall with a float, face down, arms and legs fully extended, i.e., a push and glide
- as above, without a float, with leg kick
- as above with small sculling movements with the arms almost fully extended
- as above, with bigger arm movements underwater, gradually introducing Front Paddle arm action

Arm Action
- continue as in leg action practices with emphasis on more powerful, longer arm actions
- shallow water, standing one foot in advance of the other, upper body leaning forward, copying teacher/coach demonstration of the arm action
- as above, face in the water
- push and glide, introduce leg action and then add arm action
- repeat, increasing distances covered

Breathing
- standing, nose and lips in the water, blowing bubbles
- repeat, emphasis on exhalation
- short distances, full stroke, breathing once, twice etc

Timing of the stroke (co-ordination)
- head up Front Crawl watching hands enter the water and extend forwards
- single arm action, the other arm supported by a float, to concentrate on the correction of a particular arm fault (use this practice/drill sparingly with inexperienced swimmers)
- "catch up" Front Crawl – arms extended in front of the head. One arm executes an arm stroke, whilst the other remains static in the extended position. It is important to retain the constant kicking pattern throughout this stroke (again, use sparingly with inexperienced swimmers)

Major faults and their possible causes and some examples of corrective measures

Fault	Cause	Correction
Low hips or legs	Head too high through: ● fear of placing face in water ● mistaken idea of head position ● inability to master breathing technique ● incorrect breathing action	● ensure forehead and face are down in the water ● return to confidence practices if necessary
Snaking movements of the body	● hands entering the water across the body mid-line ● incorrect hand/arm pathways underwater	● on entry, place hands mid-way between shoulder and head
Excessive body roll	● turning the head too far on breathing ● hands entering the water across the body mid-line	● keep one goggle or eye in the water when breathing
Loss of power to arm stroke	● dropped elbow, i.e., allowing the elbow to fall below the hand	● ensure the elbow remains 'high' throughout the stroke
Short arm stroke	● short upsweep	● ensure hand sculls through all the way to the thigh
Feet or lower legs coming out of the water resulting in a wasted leg action	● head too low ● excessive bending of the knees ● poor ankle mobility	● full stroke concentrating on legs and adjusting the head position to keep hips below the surface ● use exercises to mobilise the joint ● consider the need for greater stress on arm action with legs used mainly for balance

Chapter 12

Back Crawl

Bill Furniss

Introduction

Back Crawl, as the name implies, is performed on the back (supine position). The limb actions for the stroke are of the alternating type. In historical terms there have been many techniques for swimming on the back. The two most used methods, before the alternating "crawl" type movements were adopted, were known as the Elementary Backstroke and the (Old) English Backstroke. Details will found in Endpiece to Part IV.

Gradually, swimmers started to use an alternating arm action. First of all it was done with an inverted Breaststroke kick, but swimmers very quickly realised the advantage of kicking the legs in an alternating fashion and the first signs of the Backstroke, as we know it today, began to emerge. Backstroke received its recognition when, in 1906, for international competitions, three strokes were recognised – Breaststroke, Freestyle and Backstroke. At first, in Backstroke races, the Old English, Elementary and the new alternating technique were used, but in a very short space of time the alternating stroke proved its superiority and, by 1912, was used almost exclusively by all backstrokers and became known as the Back Crawl.

General description of the stroke

The swimmer is supine and in a streamlined position. The arms recover over the water in what is sometimes called a "windmilling" action. The leg kick is of the alternating type.

Detail of the stroke

Body position

General

The body should be on the back in a flat, horizontal and streamlined position. However, there has to be enough inclination from the head to the feet to allow the legs to operate during the kick without breaking the surface of the water. Benefits of the horizontal body position in terms of reducing the drag are obvious, but not so obvious is the importance of a good streamlined body position. Back Crawl is an alternating stroke and there is always the danger of the body moving from side to side in the water (lateral deviation or sway) (See Fig. 12.1). Basically, the proficient Back Crawl exponent should maintain two straight lines, one horizontal and one streamlined, if drag is to be minimized.

Head

The position of the head is critical if the correct body position is to be

Figure 12.1 The danger of lateral deviation.

achieved and maintained. It should be held back with the ears submerged and the eyes looking upwards. Some successful Back Crawl swimmers hold their heads in a higher position than this. Generally, these swimmers have exceptional buoyancy, flexibility and very good kicks. The most important single point to stress is that the head should be held perfectly still at all times during the stroke.

Hips

The hips should ride reasonably high throughout the stroke. The tendency for less able performers to "sit down" and let the hips sink should be discouraged.

Body roll around the long axis

As will be evident, when the arm action is discussed later, it is of paramount importance that the body rolls along its long axis during the stroke. The only part of the body not involved in this rotation is the head, which, as mentioned previously, should be perfectly still at all times. Three main advantages of the rotation of the body around the long axis are:

- it puts the shoulder of the arm which is recovering clear of the water so that the arm can be recovered more easily
- the arm which is providing propulsion is lowered into the water by the body's rotation, and so places it at a better angle mechanically from which to apply its propulsive force
- by placing the arm, which is providing propulsion, down into the water, and the shoulder of the recovery arm out of the water, a more streamlined body position is achieved.

Leg action

General

All good Back Crawl swimmers need strong, efficient leg kicks. Basically the kick is a six beat action, and is mainly used for balance. It is unlikely that most swimmers will derive a significant amount of propulsion from the kick. For exceptional "kickers" the small amount that would be achieved would be most effective when the arms were not in the propulsive phase, i.e., when one arm is above the head at entry and the other arm is by the side having just finished its pull. The fact that the kick is used mainly for balance does not mean it is unimportant. The job of the kick is to maintain a good body position, and to balance the strong sweeping actions made by the arms.

Path of the kick

Although the kick will be described in two parts, i.e., upkick and downkick, (sometimes described as the upbeat and downbeat) it is important to realise that the kick does not actually take place in a vertical plane. We have already ascertained that the body rolls around its long axis during the stroke and that this is a beneficial movement. Obviously, if the body is rolling from side to side, then so are the hips. The path of the kick is, therefore, influenced by the relationship of the hips to the body roll at the time of the upkick or downkick.

Upkick

At the commencement of the upkick the leg is below the level of the hip and in a reasonably straight position with the foot slightly turned up (dorsiflexed). This position of the foot is often overlooked since we only really need a stretched (plantarflexed) position on the upkick. From this position the upkick is initiated by flexion of the hip which in turn raises the upper leg, this is followed almost simultaneously by flexion of the knee joint and then, just after that, by the movement of the ankle which places the foot in the desired extended (plantarflexed) position. Many swimmers will also slightly "in-toe" at this point. The leg should continue upwards, with the foot pointed, in a smooth accelerating fashion in which the swimmer should feel the kick travelling through hips, thigh, knee and foot. The acceleration of the lower leg and foot is of great importance in effective kicking. The upkick ends when the leg is completely extended at the knee with the toes close to the water surface.

Downkick

Once the upkick is completed the muscular effort should cease and the leg should be straight but relaxed. It will then start downwards quite naturally. The leg will remain in a straight position, with the foot relaxed and the toes pointing upwards, until near the end of the downkick when the leg is below the hip and the upkick is ready to start again. The depth of the leg at this point is approximately 45cms. As one leg finishes the upkick the other should be at the end of the downkick. It will be apparent from the above that ankle flexibility is of considerable importance to the Back Crawl swimmer.

Arm action

The Back Crawl uses an alternating windmilling action of the arms. The propulsive underwater action is followed by an out of the water recovery. The importance of powerful propulsive movements during the underwater section is obvious, but the teacher/coach needs to stress the importance of correct recovery actions in order to avoid excessive body movements and, therefore, reduce resistance.

Entry

The hand enters the water, little finger first, in advance of the head and approximately in line with the shoulder. The arm is fully extended, but without any undue tension. It is important that the swimmer does not overreach at this point. The palm of the hand should be facing outward and the hand should then sink to a depth of about 30cms, causing the minimum amount of drag. This sinking action is natural because of body roll, and the side the hand is on will be rolling into the water at this time. The importance of entering the hand in line with the shoulder should be stressed. Entries too close to the midline, or too wide of it, will have detrimental effects on streamlining and propulsion. The importance of the little finger entry should also be stressed. Swimmers who enter with the back of the hand cause more resistance and cannot sink the hand effectively to the desired position. Furthermore, there is often a tendency to commence the pull with the little finger leading. The hand feels for the pressure of the water in preparation for the sweeping propulsive movements which are to follow. Shortly after the hand "fixes" (catch) on the water the palm is rotated so that it faces downwards. When the swimmer presses on the water the elbow will bend (flex) and the upper arm rotate. This gives the high elbow position required to enable the initial downward sweep to be performed effectively.

Downsweep

From the catch position the hand sweeps in a downward and outward path, reaching a depth of approximately 50cms. The pulling side of the body will roll towards the sweeping hand at this time which, together with the now lower, flexed elbow position, gives the impression of leaning into the stroke to provide a desirable, strong, propulsive action.

Pitch of the hand

It is important to realise that swimmers will continually alter the pitch of the hand throughout the sweeping actions. In order to get the best possible propulsive results during the downsweep the hand should be pitched downwards, outwards and slightly backwards.

112

Upsweep

Once the hand reaches a depth of approximately 50cms it starts to sweep in an upward direction and eventually an upward, backward and inward direction. During the upsweep the flexion of the elbow joint increases and, by the time this upward movement ends, the flexion of the elbow should have reached approximately 90 degrees, although this angle varies from swimmer to swimmer. If the teacher/coach views the swimmer from the side at this point the underwater propulsive phase of the hand appears to be half completed. The pitch of the hand is obviously in the same direction as that of the sweeping action, i.e., upwards and inwards. At the completion of the upsweep the hand is just below the surface of the water with the fingers facing diagonally upwards and outwards.

Second downsweep

The pitch of the hand is now changed from upwards to downwards and slightly sidewards. The hand then sweeps downwards and inwards in an accelerating fashion with the elbow extending throughout the movement. When the hand reaches the end of the downward and inward movement the arm is fully extended, with the hand below the hip and the arm close to the hip and upper thigh.

Figure 12.2 The "S" shaped pull.

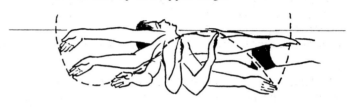

The "S" shaped pull pattern

When viewed from the side the movements made by the hand as it sweeps against the water, resemble an "S" shape when laid on its side. (Fig. 12.2).

The importance of the downsweep and body roll

The final downward sweeping action of the hand, when done with acceleration and force, pushes the shoulder of the same side of the body up and so initiates body roll. At the same time the other arm which is recovering, is falling towards the water, thus assisting the rolling action. If good body roll is to be achieved the importance of a good strong downward sweeping action must be stressed.

The importance of hand acceleration

Once the initial catch is made the Back Crawl swimmer should accelerate the hand continuously throughout the sweeping movement.

Recovery

When the body rolls after the final downsweep of the hand the recovery action of the arm commences. The hand of the arm about to recover is below the level of the hip and so needs to be lifted through the water in a way which causes the swimmer the minimum amount of resistance. This is achieved by rotating the hand inwards so the palm faces the thigh, the hand can then cut through the water on its side. As it is brought up it will leave the water thumb first. Another type of recovery by the hand is to flex the wrist in a relaxed movement so the hand can leave the water with the back of the hand uppermost and the fingers pointing down. Either of these methods is acceptable, with the former being the preferred method. After leaving the water the arms should be brought directly over the shoulder which should be in an elevated position due to the body roll. As the hand is thumb up, or back of the hand up, the arm is rotated gradually from the shoulder joint to place the hand in a little finger entry position as it passes the head on its way down into the water. The arm should be straight and relaxed during the recovery so that the muscles of the arms can recover from their propulsive effort. The swimmer should not overreach at this time.

Arm opposition

The timing of the recovery and propulsive arm position is vital to good technique. Basically, as the recovering arm enters the water the propulsive arm should be sweeping down at the end of its propulsive phase. The opposition of the arms helps such factors as body roll and streamlining as well as providing the most continuous application of propulsive force on the water.

Breathing

As the face is clear of the water breathing is not a major problem. Basically, the timing of the breathing is to inhale on the recovery of one arm and exhale on the recovery of the opposite arm.

Timing of the stroke (co-ordination)

In the description of the leg action the term six beat kick was used, i.e., each leg kicks diagonally upwards three times during one complete arm cycle. The first diagonal upkick occurs during the time the arm on the same side is sweeping down at the start of its propulsive effort. The second diagonal upkick occurs during the upward sweeping movement of the opposite arm. The third diagonal upkick occurs during the downsweep by the arm on the same side. This sequence is repeated by the leg of the opposite side to give us our six beat kick.

Figure 12.3 Full Back Crawl sequence – commencing at left hand entry. Shown from side view, head on and slightly below.

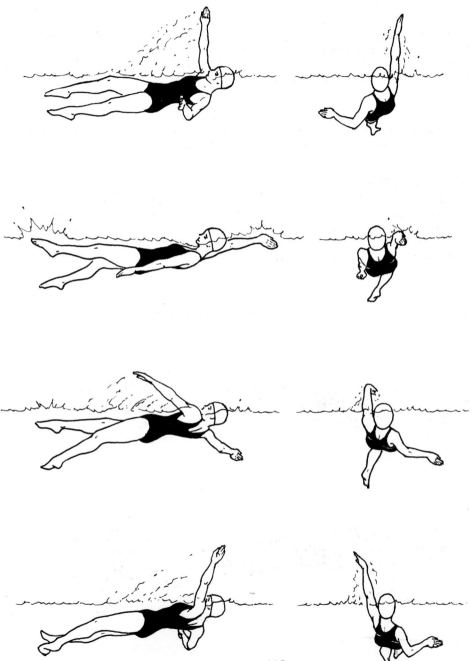

Teaching/coaching points

The fundamentals of the stroke are:

Body position

- flat, streamlined, horizontal – keep the body as close to the flat position as possible and avoid piking or sitting down at the hips
- vertical streamlining, (i.e., as seen from above) – check that the body does not sway from side to side
- body roll – swimmers should roll around the long axis
- still head – a good still head position is very important, particularly under stress

Leg action

- fast, even kicking
- lateral kicking – emphasise the relationship of the kick with the body roll and the need to balance the sideways movements of the stroke
- point the toes – stress importance of good ankle flexibility and the ability to point (plantarflex) the toes on the upkick
- reduce knee bend – although the swimmer needs to bend the knee during the kick the teacher/coach should continually check that the knee bend on the upkick is not excessive, particularly with young swimmers during the early stages of learning

Arm action

- little finger entry – the teacher/coach should stress this type of entry and check that the hand sinks to the required depth prior to starting the propulsive phase
- sweep the hand – swimmers should be taught to move the hand in a sweeping type of action in order to develop the correct "S" shaped pattern
- higher elbow position – the swimmer cannot actually see this action because of the relative position of the head and arm. The teacher/coach should, therefore, continually check for this position at the start of the propulsive action
- press down at the end of the propulsive phase – swimmers should be encouraged to press straight down towards the bottom of the pool at the end of the propulsive phase to encourage body roll
- acceleration – swimmers should be coached for an accelerating, sweeping action of the hands throughout the movement under the water

Recovery

- release from the water – thumb first, or back of the hand with fingers pointing downwards
- relaxed recovery – the absence of tension during recovery is common amongst good swimmers and should be encouraged. Swimmers should be discouraged from overreaching

Timing

- fast legs, smooth arms – the teacher/coach should stress the speed of the kick whilst at the same time controlling the tempo of the arm stroke

Breathing

- inhale on one arm, exhale on the other arm

Stroke practices/drills for Back Crawl

Swimming on the back, and therefore, unable to see where one is going, is not a natural situation. Practices/drills are vital if the complete Back Crawl swimmer is to be produced.

Body position practices/drills
- use of Back Paddle stroke to emphasize body position
- push and glide on back – effect, develops flat, horizontal position
- push and glide on side – introduces swimmer to the position they will be in at the maximum degree of body roll
- kicking with one arm along the water above the head – effect, as above but will get the swimmer used to the feel of correct body position with the arms in the position of "opposition" required in good technique

Kicking and body roll practices/drills
- kicking, float held on abdomen or thighs
- six kicks, lift right shoulder – effect, develops six beat kick and body roll, arms should be kept by the side during this drill
- six kicks, lift left shoulder – effect, as above
- kicking and single arm – effect, develops body roll to side of pulling arm and better feel of kick. Arm not in use is held alongside the body
- vertical kicking – in deep water, Back Crawl kicking in a vertical position – effect, develops strength of kick

Arm practices/drills
- double arm swimming – effect, easier to work the "S" shaped action plus entry and finish and acceleration through the stroke
- pulling with buoy – effect, develops muscular endurance in arms and feel of arm action (not for early Back Crawl swimmers)
- short to long stroke – swimmers enter at a line opposite the shoulder and then as they progress down the pool they gradually reach further back until entering in the correct position. Effect, gradually develops feel of sweeping actions
- Back Paddle for short distance, then introduce Back Crawl arm action

Timing practices/drills
Practices/drills for timing in the stroke involve a variety of combinations of one arm swimming with the leg action, e.g., three left arm, three right arm, two left, two right, one left, one right, etc. Effect, to develop a strong kick with body roll and help the arms to fit into the stroke at the desired time during the leg kicks.

Use of flippers
Many of the practices/drills above can be performed with flippers. They are of particular use to the inexperienced swimmer, or on drills where a high degree of efficiency is required to perform the action correctly.

Major faults their possible causes and some examples of corrective measures

Fault	Cause	Correction
Hips too low	● head too high or piking of the body ● lack of confidence	● place head further back ● encourage hip lift ● return to early practices
Legs too low	● head too high ● poor leg action	● place head back ● check leg action
Knees breaking water surface	● excessive bending of the knees during kick (cycling)	● teach kick with straighter legs ● legs only practices with 1 or 2 floats
Kicking with feet dorsiflexed	● lack of mobility in ankle joint ● poor understanding of foot position	● flexibility exercises ● in extreme cases teach a more arm dominated stroke ● kick with toes pointed/stretched
Kick too shallow	● lack of understanding of the potential contribution of the kick to the stroke	● emphasise slower, and deeper kick. When correct depth is achieved increase speed of leg action once more
Back of hand entry	● lack of appreciation of little finger entry ● trying to turn hand over for entry at too late a point	● out of water practice to teach rotation of the arms from shoulder girdle to achieve little finger entry position
Starting to pull too soon	● lack of understanding ● lack of shoulder flexibility	● emphasize that the hand should sink prior to starting propulsive phase ● shoulder flexibility exercises and single arm backstroke with one arm by the side to develop sinking action of the hand and sinking action of the body to the propulsive side
Elbow not below level of hand	● lack of strength ● lack of understanding	● strength practices if required ● double arm drill emphasising lower elbow position
Not pressing down at finish	● lack of understanding ● swimmers think they are pushing the water back and are not sweeping effectively	● double arm practices ● emphasis on strong, accelerating press down at finish

118

Bobbing or jerking of body action and lateral sway	● rushing recovery ● overreaching or ineffective leg action ● inaccurate arm path underwater	● practices for loose, relaxed recovery, e.g., full stroke with flippers so that swimmers can concentrate on recovery without rushing the stroke ● for reducing lateral sway, leg practices kicking on the back or side to develop diagonal direction of up kick ● check arm pathway under water
Hands entering too wide	● lack of appreciation of entry position ● lack of shoulder mobility	● encourage exaggerated entry position i.e., on or over the centre line of progression ● swing the arm over the shoulder ● shoulder mobilising exercises in extreme cases
Hands stopping at thighs	● failure to appreciate the continuous windmilling nature of action	● stress the "lift out" action ● stress continuity of movement without pauses

Chapter 13

The Breaststroke

Bill Furniss

Introduction

Breaststroke is the oldest of the competitive strokes and, also, the slowest of the four major strokes used today. At the highest level it is very definitely a "specialist stroke" and, yet, at the learner stage, it seems to be as easy as the Front Crawl or Back Crawl to master. Because Breaststroke has always been the slowest of the competitive strokes swimmers and coaches have constantly looked for ways to increase its speed and efficiency. Technical descriptions of the stroke can be found in publications dated as early as the 16th century. However, by the middle of the 18th century the "wedgekick", using a wide sweeping action by the legs, became popular and remained so for many years.

In 1906, when swimming competition was split into 3 styles in Great Britain, Breaststroke, for the first time, had a set of rules. In 1925 various swimming periodicals described the long, sideways pull of the arms as being replaced by a shorter pull which enabled a faster sequence of movements to be introduced. So, then, we have the first mention of increasing the stroke tempo. Further ways of improving speed led to the development of the Butterfly stroke in the 1930s. This started when Breaststroke swimmers, because of a weakness in the drafting of the laws, began to pull their arms down to their thighs then swing them forward over the water. This development of the stroke caused confusion, and not a little animosity, eventually leading FINA, the world governing body of swimming, to recognise Butterfly as a stroke in its own right in 1935. The situation of both Breaststroke and Butterfly being used in the same race, however, continued for some years, and it was not until 1952 that the strokes were split into separate events. By the 1950s swimmers were experimenting with a much faster Breaststroke and were reducing the glide.

Underwater Breaststroke

After the Butterfly and Breaststroke were split into separate competitive events there was nothing in the rules to prevent Breaststrokers from swimming some or all of the stroke under water. Once more, swimmers and coaches looked for new ways to increase speed in the stroke. The solution was to swim some of the stroke under water. The Japanese, in particular, did lots of work with this type of stroke and, in the 1956 Olympic Games, the 200 metre Breaststroke event was won by Masura Furukaua in a time of 2 mins 34.7 secs. He swam much of the race submerged. Following the 1956 Olympic Games the rules were changed to exclude underwater swimming apart from one long pull and kick after the dive and turn. More recently the "head under" law has been refined to remedy some inconsistencies.

General description of the stroke

There are two main variations in use by swimmers today:
- the flat stroke – when the shoulders stay in the water for most of the stroke cycle and the body remains in a relatively, flat stable position

● high lift stroke – in which the shoulders are lifted high out of the water in an upward and forward motion as the insweep of the arm stroke is made.

The preference for which type of variation is to be used is usually left to the individual swimmer. Such factors as body type, strength, flexibility etc., will determine the appropriate type of stroke, and the teacher/coach should try to encourage the development of a natural technique.

Detail of the stroke

Body position

The body should be as flat, streamlined and horizontal as possible with enough inclination from the head to the feet to allow the recovery of the legs to take place without bringing the lower part of the legs out of the water. This description would be fine for swimmers using the flat stroke but, clearly, swimmers using the high lift stroke will need a more inclined position at the front of the body during the lifting part of the stroke. Generally, swimmers who use the latter technique have excellent lower back flexibility and can keep the hips and legs in a streamlined position during the lifting movement.

Important points to remember are:
● during the propulsive phase of the arm stroke the hips should be as close to the surface of the water as possible with the legs in line with the body
● the upper body and face should be in the water and streamlined during the propulsive kick back of the legs. In general, when one end of the body is providing the propulsive force the other end should stay as streamlined as possible.

Leg action

Most Breaststroke swimmers now use the narrow, backward, around and downward kick, called the whip kick. The wider sweeping wedge action is virtually discontinued as a competitive stroke. However, many recreational swimmers find it a useful, relaxing stroke to swim, and it also has some use in lifesaving. Unlike the alternating strokes, where the leg action is mainly used for balance and provides very little propulsion for most swimmers, the leg action in Breaststroke is propulsive. The effectiveness of the propulsive phase depends on the power, speed of limb movement and a sweeping action by the feet on the water. The danger facing the Breaststroker is that, whilst the kick is propulsive, the recovery phase of the kick creates resistance. The Breaststroke swimmer has to ensure that:
● the recovery of the legs is streamlined, whilst at the same time being able to place them in a good position to start the kick (propulsive) phase
● the development of the limb track during the kick back enables the feet to effectively sweep against the water in a powerful, accelerating movement.

Leg recovery

With the legs extended and straight, following the kick back, the recovery is initiated by the lowering of the hips which corresponds with the finish of the insweep of the arm stroke. At this point the upper body is lifting as the swimmer breathes, so it is natural for the hips to go down at this time. The knees and hips are relaxed and the upper legs are then brought forwards and slightly outwards by flexion of the knees and flexion and outward rotation of the hips. The feet at this time should be pointing backwards and plantarflexed and should slightly turn in (in-toe) in order to reduce drag. As the feet approach the buttocks they should turn up and out (dorsiflex and evert) in preparation for the start of the propulsive phase. Most good Breaststroke swimmers tend not to bring the upper legs too far forward. Rather, they move the upper legs minimally and bring the lower legs up which gives a far more streamlined position as indicated in Fig. 13.1, and yet still places the feet in an excellent position to kick back. The optimum hip flexion, i.e., the angle made between the trunk and the thighs, would appear to be 125-135 degrees, although the range might start at 110 degrees in the early stages of swimming. As the upper legs are brought forwards the knees also part slightly. The width of the knees on recovery depends on the individual, but generally too wide a position of the knees would be detrimental to good stroke mechanics with the maximum spread of the knees being just outside hip width.

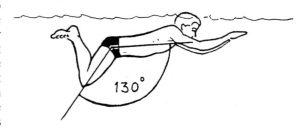

Figure 13.1 Angles for hip flexion.

The propulsive phase

During the propulsive phase of the kick the swimmer is trying to move his feet in an outward, backward and eventually downward direction so that the feet have the best opportunity to fix on the water in a sweeping, driving action. At the end of the leg recovery the hips and knees are flexed and the feet are close to the buttocks in a dorsiflexed and everted position. The kick starts with the feet moving in an outward, backward direction in a sweeping movement. No propulsion occurs during the first few centimetres of the kick but, eventually, the feet "catch" the water and the propulsive phase commences. The knees and hips continue to extend as force is applied during the sweeping movements of the feet. Towards the end of the knee and hip extension the path of the kick changes to not only a backwards sweep but also an inward and downward sweep. The kick nears completion when the legs are fully extended. Some swimmers will finish with the feet touching at this point, although most finish with a space between the feet which can be almost as wide as hip width. The swimmers who finish in this position will then bring the feet together in a strong, insweeping action, and it is important to impress on the swimmer the need for acceleration throughout the propulsive phase of the leg action. The feet start the kick slowly through "catch", and then there is progressive acceleration through the rest of the kick, eventually finishing in a whip-like action. Once the feet are together the muscular effort in the legs is relaxed and the legs are now fully extended with the feet plantarflexed once more. They are then allowed to rise to the same level as the hips in a streamlined position.

Arm action

The purpose of the arm action is to create as much propulsion as possible by using the hands in a sweeping type movement against the water. Basically, the sweeping path the hands should take is outwards, downwards and inwards; after these movements have been made the arms are stretched forward into the recovery action.

Outsweep – catch – downsweep

After the recovery the arms should be in a relaxed, fully extended position. The thumbs should be touching with the fingers pointing forward and the inside of the elbows close together. The first movement by the swimmer is to "pitch the hands". This will vary slightly from swimmer to swimmer but, generally, the hands turn so that the thumbs are lower than the rest of the hand and the palms are facing diagonally downwards and outwards. The swimmer next starts to sweep the hands outwards, at first with very little pressure, so that the hands can "feel" the water. As this action progresses the pressure and speed of the movement increases. The outward sweeping action continues until "catch" is reached and the hands fix on the water. From here the propulsive phase proper commences. The exact point of the catch can vary from swimmer to swimmer but, generally, it takes place when the hands are approximately shoulder width apart. As the hands have also been moving diagonally downwards they will be about 15-22cms below the surface at this point. At catch several things happen which are fundamental to good technique. Firstly, the hands change pitch so they are pressing outwards, downwards and backwards. Secondly, the arms start to bend and, thirdly, the shoulders rotate inwards. These changes give the swimmer the "high elbow" position needed in all prone strokes for truly efficient swimming. Eventually the hands are pointing downwards and the hands reach the deepest point in their downward sweeping action.

Insweep
The circular motion the hands changes from sweeping downwards to sweeping inwards as they approach their deepest point. The hands sweep inwards, upwards and slightly backwards as the acceleration throughout the stroke is maintained. The inward sweeping action provides a considerable amount of propulsion, so the maintenance of the pressure on the hands and their acceleration is important. The path of the elbows will follow that made by the hands, but generally they should be brought inwards towards the chest wall (see Fig. 13.2). As the hands near the end of the inward sweeping action the elbows should not be allowed to pull back behind the line of the shoulder. If this occurred it would cause a loss of propulsive force and, more importantly, an increase in resistance. The hands should be in the position indicated in Fig. 13.3. Most good swimmers on this stroke sweep the hands inwards and slightly forwards ahead of the elbows, towards the end of the sweeping action. This provides more propulsion and facilitates the desired elbow position.

Recovery
The completion of the insweep brings the hands together under the chin. The hands have been accelerating all the time up to this point and the swimmer needs to control the first part of the recovery action so that a smooth transition from the end of the insweep to the start of the recovery is achieved. The arms and hands are generally stretched forwards in the most streamlined fashion possible, and the pitch of the hands is altered once more so that they face palm downwards by the time the action is completed. At the end of the action the arms should be in a relaxed and fully extended position.

Figure 13.2 Sweeping movement for the arms.   *Figure 13.3 Commencement of the recovery.*

Breathing
Breathing in Breaststroke is usually not a problem. The head is clear of the water at the time the hands finish the insweep and are directly under the chin. All Breaststroke swimmers should breathe in at this point; as the arms recover the head is lowered into the water. During the underwater sweeping action of the armstroke the aim is to gradually exhale so that the final exhalation of air is made as the mouth breaks the surface of the water.

Timing of the stroke (co-ordination)

The timing in Breaststroke, put simply, is that when the legs are kicking back, the front of the body is as streamlined as possible; when the arms are providing propulsion, the back end of the body is as streamlined as possible. Certain variations in timing occur based on the swimmer's individuality, e.g., some swimmers have a "glide" orientated stroke whilst others have a stroke with a much faster tempo. Both, however, use the same basics as above, the difference being the amount of time they keep their bodies in the streamlined position. Beginners and young swimmers usually start by learning the glide type of timing and, as they become more experienced, they can develop their own tempo based on trial and error.

Glide timing

The arms start the propulsive phase with the legs remaining fully extended behind. As the arms start the insweep the legs start to recover by flexion of the knees and hips. When the arms finish the insweep the legs should be fully recovered. The kickback is delayed slightly until the arms are about two thirds of the way forward in their recovery movement. At this point the legs start their drive so that by the time the arms are fully extended in front, and the head is in the water after breathing, the leg action begins its propulsive phase.

Figure 13.4 Full Breaststroke sequence – commencing at full stretch glide. Shown from side view, head on and slightly below.

Teaching/coaching points

When teaching/coaching the Breaststroke certain fundamentals need emphasis. These give the basic stroke around which the individual swimmer's technique will develop.

Body position

- keep the body as flat as possible during the kick phase
- keep the lift natural. A high lift stroke should be a natural reaction to the strong insculling (swirling) of the arms and not a deliberate attempt to copy another swimmer who appears to be successful
- lift the shoulders up and forward. Clearly, lifting the shoulders up and back would present the whole of the chest to the oncoming water. It would not be a very streamlined position
- keep the head still. The head comes up because the shoulders lift and no independent movement of the head needs to take place.

Pull

- sweep and circle – pressing movements in a circular fashion, outwards, downwards, inwards and upwards, should be encouraged
- feel for the pressure on the hands. Swimmers should be encouraged to feel the pressure on the last two fingers of their hands, particularly on the insweep
- bring the shoulders forwards and keep the high elbow position. With weak swimmers rotation of the shoulders, and the corresponding high elbow position during the end of the outsweep, needs to be stressed continuously. Many swimmers can keep quite a flat position of the arms at this point and can still generate lift if they are powerful enough
- acceleration – swimmers should be taught/coached to accelerate throughout the sweeping action once the initial pressure on the hands is achieved
- deceleration – as the arms are pushed in front of the body during the recovery the movement is slow and carefully controlled
- elbows in – at the end of the insweep, prior to the recovery, the elbows are tucked into a position close to the chest
- elbows in front of the shoulders – throughout the arm action the elbows should remain in front of the shoulder line.

Leg action

- fast feet (acceleration) – the kick should be accelerated once the initial pressure on the feet is felt
- heels up and knees back – this will reduce resistance and retardation
- keep it narrow – again for reduced resistance
- kick back and **down** – this helps the natural dolphin action of the hips

Timing

- wait for the kick back – emphasise the wait for the kick until the hands are pushed about two thirds of the way forward in the recovery of the arms
- glide – the glide phase of the stroke is important, even though some fast tempo swimmers might reduce this to a minimum when they are competing.

Breathing

- breathe out at the end of the pull – breathing out occurs at the end of the sweeping action. No independent movement of the head is necessary.

126

Stroke practices/drills for Breaststroke

There are many practices/drills available for Breaststroke swimmers. Whilst variety is important for maintaining interest, effective motor learning requires frequent repetition of known activities.

Kicking practices/drills

- kick with float/board (in prone position) – effect, develops leg strength and local muscular endurance
- kick on the back – effect, develops the ability to drop the lower leg on the recovery whilst keeping the upper legs reasonably still
- kick arms in front – effect, develops good kick with body in glide position
- kick with a band above the knees – effect, development of narrow kick with knees held together (Not for early Breaststrokers)
- treading water – effect, develops strength of legs and sculling action of feet.

Pulling practices/drills

- standing, shallow water, upper body horizontal, attempt arm action
- building – start with small sweeping actions, gradually increasing the width of sweep, These practices/drills can be done with a float between the legs or by using Front Crawl leg kick or Butterfly kick – effect, develops natural sweeping action in both inward and outward movements
- pull board/buoy – effect, develops strength and local muscular endurance in arms
- alternating pull action of either arm (arm not being used is kept in front in the glide position) – effect, more effective sweep developed with just the one arm. With the head up the mechanics of the arm pull can be watched more carefully(not for early Breaststrokers)

Timing practices/drills

Timing practices/drills deserve considerable attention. An example of such a practice/drill is, say, two kicks – one pull, or two pulls – one kick. A variation might be three kicks – one pull, two kicks – two pull, one kick – three pulls, etc.

Major faults, their possible causes and some examples of corrective measures

Fault	Cause	Correction
Screw kick (Uneven or asymmetrical kick)	<ul><li>not turning the offending foot or feet out and up as the leg kick is made (everting and dorsiflexing)</li><li>possibly inaccurate head/shoulder position</li></ul>	<ul><li>encourage the swimmer to pull the toe towards the shin at the beginning of the kick phase</li><li>try Breaststroke kicking on the back so that the swimmer can watch the foot action</li><li>check body position in general</li></ul>
Knee brought forwards on the recovery too much	<ul><li>misunderstanding of the use of the lower legs and feet in the propulsive phase</li></ul>	<ul><li>Various drills/practices e.g., Breaststroke kick and hands by the side to touch heels or Breaststroke kick on the back dropping the lower legs to develop the feel for this type of recovery</li></ul>

Incorrect limb track, e.g., kick directed in backward plane only	● misunderstanding of the sweeping action of the feet	● various drill/practices, e.g., treading water to develop feel of the sweeping action with the feet ● dolphin kick drill/practice alternating with the Breaststroke kick to develop the downward action of the kick
Dropped elbow on pull or poor outsweep	● not medially rotating the shoulders ● not holding the pressure on the hands during the outward press	● lots of sweeping drills/practices, e.g., sweeping Breaststroke actions with Front Crawl kick. (Arms need to work harder and sweep more effectively to hold the water)
Poor insweep of arms plus lack of acceleration	● misunderstanding of importance of propulsive potential of this part of the arm action ● poor pitch of the hands	● again, sweeping action drills/practices to stress the importance of the acceleration of the hand and the feel of the water on the hands at this point
Poor timing	● generally rushing the stroke ● not giving time for correct alternation between pull and kick	● timing drills/practices such as 3 kicks to 1 pull, 2 kicks to 1 pull, 2 pulls to 1 kick, etc ● exaggerate the glide, e.g., swim full stroke, kick and hold the glide for say 3 seconds
Breathing too early in arms action	● incorrect timing of head lift in relation to arm sweeping action	● emphasize breathing in at the end of the insweep ● make sure the swimmer is exhaling gradually whilst the arms are performing the outward and inward sweeping action

Chapter 14

Butterfly

Nick Sellwood

Introduction

Butterfly is the second fastest competitive swimming stroke and the most recently developed of the four competitive styles. Reference to the introduction to Chapter 13 shows how the stroke evolved from Breaststroke. It is difficult to ascertain just who was the first individual to use a Butterfly type style. However, Eric Rademacher (Germany), George Kaplan (USA) and Henry Myers (USA) in 1933 are some of the earliest recorded names.

General description of the stroke

The swimmer is in a prone position moving arms and legs simultaneously and continuously. The arms recover over the water with the legs, nowadays, kicking upwards and downwards in a vertical plane. The body moves in an undulating, or dolphin, type pattern with the head rising above the water to breathe at the end of the underwater arm pull. The hands trace a series of sculling type actions in the water, sweeping outwards, downwards, inwards and finally outwards again to exit the water by the thighs.

Detail of the the stroke

Body position

The body is in the face down (prone), horizontal, streamlined position, although this position changes throughout the stroke cycle. During the most propulsive section of the stroke's arm action the body is in a level position, but during the initial outsweep of the arms, after they enter the water, and the first downkick, the hips rise upwards and forwards to break the surface. This movement is also repeated during the second kick down of the legs.

Leg action

The kick is made by a simultaneous movement upwards and downwards of the legs in a vertical plane. The legs are together with the feet plantarflexed. The kick is similar to the Front Crawl alternating kick, with the legs kept together.

Upbeat (Recovery phase)

The legs begin in an extended position with the feet plantarflexed. The hips are close to the surface at this stage. The legs simultaneously start to rise in an extended position; as they rise towards the surface the knees start to flex allowing the feet to rise further. At the same time the hips get lower in the water.

Downbeat (Propulsive phase)

From the final position described in the upbeat the feet start to 'whip' downwards past the knees in a relatively deep kick. The feet are together in a plantarflexed position, but angled slightly inwards (in-toeing). As the feet drive downwards the hips move upwards. Normally there is a two beat kicking pattern.

Arm action

Entry

The hands enter the water about shoulder width apart. The thumb and first finger enter the water first with the palms pitched outwards at about 45 degrees to the surface of the water. The arms are almost at full stretch for the entry.

Outsweep

From the entry position the arms extend forwards, downwards and slightly outwards and it is here that catch point is found. The hands reach their maximum width during this initial outsweep and the hands are pitched outwards. The elbows are kept in the high position as the pull begins.

Downsweep and insweep

As the hands reach the end of the outsweep their path changes to an inward direction and the arms then accelerate inwards and downwards. The hands reach their deepest point during the first stage of the insweep. Throughout this movement the elbows are kept higher than the hands. The hands sweep inwards and upwards coming very close together and relatively close to the abdomen. The elbows are flexed to 90 degrees during this phase.

Outsweep

The hands sweep outwards and accelerate to their fastest underwater speed. They continue until the arm is extended past the hips and the wrists rotate so that the final sculling action leaves the little finger uppermost and the palms at this point facing the thighs.

Recovery

This phase begins in the water as an extension of the final outsweep of the hands and arms. The little finger leaves the water first and continues to lead the arm recovery until just before the hands reach the shoulder level. The arms recover low and almost straight, with the hands relaxed. The elbows are slightly bent through the first half of the recovery but bend a little more in preparation for the entry.

Breathing

Breathing is carried out as the arms finish the propulsive phase. It is at this point that the shoulders and head rise forwards out of the water and the breath can be taken. The swimmer should extend the chin forwards in order to breathe rather than lift the head up. The chin remains close to the surface of the water and is 'snapped down' in line with the body once the breathing action is completed. The most common breathing patterns used are either to breathe every second stroke or every single stroke. The type of breathing may depend on the distance to be swum and the speed to be achieved. However, no matter which pattern is adopted, it is vital that the swimmer relates it to the stroke rhythm being used. Reference was made to the 'explosive' and 'trickle' breathing techniques in Chapter 11, The Front Crawl Stroke. The type used depends on personal preference, although the tendency amongst competitive swimmers is to use the explosive breathing pattern.

Timing of the stroke (co-ordination)

As already indicated, Butterfly is normally swum with two leg kicks to one complete cycle of the arms.

First downbeat – this occurs during the hand entry and outsweep. The downbeat is completed as the catch occurs.

First upbeat – this takes place as the downsweep and insweep of the arms occur.

Second downbeat – the timing of this co-ordinates with the upsweep of the arms.

Second upbeat – this occurs as the arms go through their recovery phase.

General observations on timing and co-ordination

The leg kick is often known as a "Major-Minor" action, emphasizing the first downbeat. However, some observers feel that the "Major" element is that the actual propulsive power being generated is greater, because it coincides with a level, more streamlined, body position, rather than the first downbeat being stronger than the second, i.e., the two downbeats could be equal.

Figure 14.1 Full Butterfly sequence – commencing at hand entry. Shown from side view, head on and slightly below.

Teaching/coaching points

Leg action
- **upbeat** – legs start extended with feet stretched
  - legs rise together and start to bend at the knees
- **downbeat** – from flexed position, simultaneous drive downwards from the surface with the feet passing the knees to an extended position

Breathing
- keep the chin close to the surface of the water
- push the chin forward to breathe then 'snap' the head down

Arm action
- **entry** – hands enter shoulder width
  - arms almost straight
  - thumb and first finger enter first, palm at about 45 degrees to the water surface
- **outsweep** – hands scull forwards and outwards
  - keep elbows high
- **downsweep and insweep** – hands angle inwards and accelerate
  - keep elbows higher than hands
  - fingers point towards each other and almost touch
- **outsweep** – hands continue to accelerate and extend past the hip
  - at the end of outsweep scull inwards
- **recovery** – little finger exits water first
  - arms recover close to the water and are relatively straight
  - elbows slightly flexed in preparation for entry

132

Stroke practices/drills
- from a standing position on the bottom of the pool the swimmer executes a dolphin type dive
- as above, but as swimmer surfaces start leg kick
- as above, but introduce an underwater arm pull and reach forward
- repeat above, but with single arm Butterfly building up the distance and number of strokes executed; carefully monitor stroke quality
- repeat above, but introduce a full arm stroke every few strokes
- introduce idea of 'kick hands in kick hands out' on arm stroke
- sculling – the swimmer tries to perform 3-5 sculling movements of the hands at the entry position, before beginning each pull

Kicking practices/drills
- from a standing position in the water, dolphin type dive and kick underwater with arms by the hips
- with float, kicking short distances
- arms outstretched, kicking across width
- repeat above but 4 kicks on the front position, 4 kicks on the side, 4 kicks lying on the back, and finally 4 kicks on the opposite side and repeat

Major faults, their possible causes and some examples of corrective measures

Fault	Cause	Correction
Arms not clearing the water on recovery	• shoulders too low in the water • lack of shoulder mobility	• keep the head and shoulders moving forwards and upwards during recovery phase • appropriate flexibility exercises • check co-ordination of leg action
Excessive resistance and retardation of forward momentum when hands enter the water	• back or palms of hands striking the water	• adjust the angle of the hand on entry and check the entry position
Hips and feet low in the water	• excessive lifting of the head on breathing	• keep chin close to the water when breathing
Excessive undulation of the body	• pushing head too deep on arm entry	• emphasis on keeping head level with shoulder line, (exaggerated correction)
Loss of propulsion on arm entry	• little or no outsweep of the hands	• introduce outsweep and slower arm action at the entry position
Loss of power to arm stroke	• 'dropped elbow' on allowing elbow to fall below hand	• ensure elbow remains 'high' throughout the stroke
Hips low as hands exit the water	• palms pushing upwards through to surface on upsweep	• introduce a rotation of wrists towards thighs ready for little finger first exit

Chapter 15

Learning to Dive

Joan Harrison

Introduction

Dives performed from springboards or highboards are a form of aerial gymnastics, a sport which combines athletic ability, body control and courage to give an aesthetically pleasing performance. The ability to enter the water from the poolside by a dive is enjoyable, it is also necessary for a good racing start and it may be an introduction to an exciting and challenging sport. The initial teaching of diving should be an integral part of swimming lessons so that there is a **safe** and gradual progression leading to the elimination of fear.

Basic principles

The success of any dive depends upon a good take-off. At take-off it is necessary to overcome inertia, and in order to do this there must be a strong push against the poolside. Frictional force is developed between the feet and the poolside which prevents the feet slipping backwards and enables the legs to extend against a fixed point. This emphasizes the importance of a good foot grip in the stance and the need to develop maximum velocity upwards and forwards. Any dive is a somersault or part of a somersault. The rotation comes from the angular momentum initiated at take-off. The flight pathway, and the angle of entry into the water, are determined at take-off and there is little that can be done to alter the body rotation whilst in flight. A strong extension of the legs gives power to the take-off, the arm swing gives a transfer of momentum of the body weight forwards. Once the feet leave the poolside the centre of gravity of the diver will follow a pre-determined path in flight. The body enters the water in a streamlined position continuing the line of flight under the water. The entry may be near vertical or at a shallow angle.

Safety factors

Diving must always be carefully supervised and the teacher/coach should impress on the class the safety factors involved so that the chances of accidents can be reduced as much as possible.

Water depth – the teacher/coach should check that there is an adequate depth of water for all underwater activities, even pushing and gliding under water can be dangerous in very shallow water. There are certain guidelines:

- head first entries from early starting positions (Crouch, Lunge) should be into water which is at least 1.8 metres deep. When pupils are learning to dive they do not automatically make a shallow entry; they are unpredictable and it is unsafe to take diving practices into shallow water
- vertical entry dives from the poolside, such as the Plain Header, require a depth of 0.5 metres DEEPER THAN THE DIVER WHEN STANDING WITH ARMS FULLY STRETCHED ABOVE THE HEAD
- Plunge or Racing Dives, which have approximately a 45° angle of entry, can be performed into 1 metre of water by a proficient diver. The learning stages, however, are more safely taken in at least a depth of 1.8 metres

- starting blocks give an elevation of 500mm to 700mm above the water level which, if used by an unskilled person, risks a steep entry into shallow water. Diving from blocks should only be introduced into a depth of at least 2.0 metres
- the height and weight of a diver must be considered because height and weight increase the velocity of travel through the water. The taller and/or heavier the diver the deeper the water needed for safety.

Pool space for diving

Care must be taken to ensure there is no danger of a diver hitting anyone in the water. This can be avoided by using an agreed diving code for the use of water space:

- a diver must always check that the entry area is clear before starting a dive. Teachers/coaches should constantly remind pupils to do this
- on resurfacing from a dive the diver should swim straight to the poolside to avoid crossing the path of another diver
- there should be no free swimming in the diving area. A rope, or rope with coloured buoys, can be used to delineate the diving area.

Class organisation and discipline

The aim throughout is to encourage pupils to take responsibility for their own actions. The teacher/coach should also explain why certain rules are being enforced:

- all diving activities in the water, or from the poolside, should be planned to enable each pupil to have a safe working space. For shallow end activities check that all pupils are safely away from the walls of the pool and are well spaced
- entries from the poolside must be carefully organised with the divers understanding the procedure. The organisation adopted by the teacher will depend upon the availability of deep water, the width of the pool, the number of divers and the activity to be performed. Figure 15.1 shows examples of how the available deep water can be organised in a safe and efficient manner.

Figure 15.1

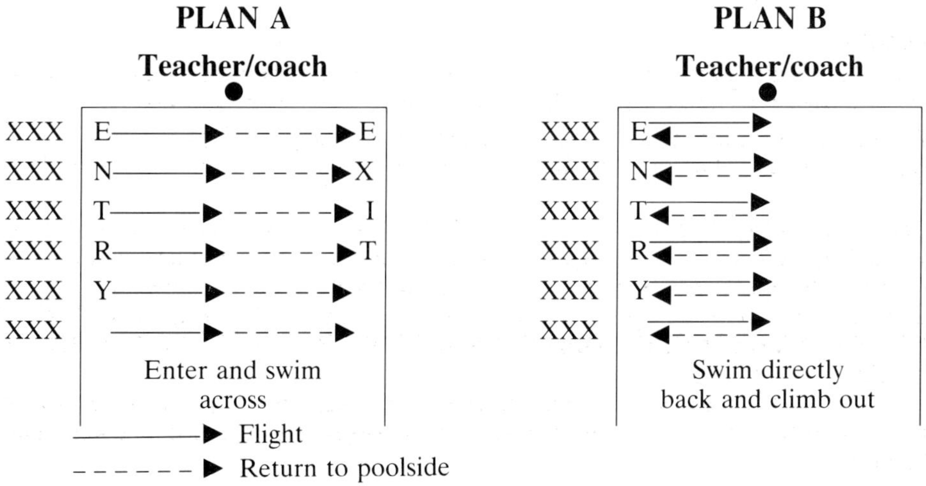

PLAN A

Teacher/coach

Enter and swim across

──────▶ Flight

- - - - - ▶ Return to poolside

PLAN B

Teacher/coach

Swim directly back and climb out

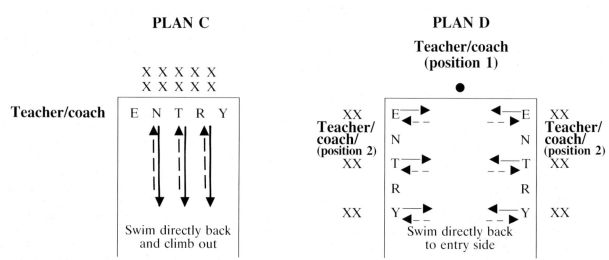

PLAN C

X X X X X
X X X X X

Teacher/coach E N T R Y

Swim directly back
and climb out

PLAN D

**Teacher/coach
(position 1)**

XX E → N T → R Y →
Teacher/
coach/
(position 2)
XX

← E N ← T R ← Y
XX
Teacher/
coach/
(position 2)
XX

Swim directly back
to entry side

Plan A

Enter, swim across the pool and climb out. This is a safe organisation, particularly when teaching a Plunge or Racing Dive. The position of the teacher/coach gives a good sideways view of the flight and entry.

Plan B

Enter and swim directly back to the side. The next diver does not go until the diver in front has touched the poolside. The teacher/coach can observe down the line and, if necessary, control the take-off for a whole line.

Plan C

The same planning as plan B, but may be used where there is a more limited area of deep water. By changing positions the teacher/coach has a closer view of, and communication with, the whole group.

Plan D

This may be adopted in a wide pool where there is no danger of divers colliding in the centre of the pool. It is a suitable plan for practices involving vertical entries, assuming, of course, the depth is appropriate.

General safety points

- divers with long hair should wear caps. Long hair coming over the face when under the water can cause panic and an unclear view. Goggles should not be worn
- by introducing diving through progressive stages the activities should be undertaken safely. Always be aware of the needs of individual pupils
- always check that the starting position is from a stance with the toes curling over the poolside. Running dives are a potential danger with the chance of slipping on a wet surface and of an uncontrolled entry
- the diver can not have a clear view of the water space available when standing back from the poolside
- a run into a dive is only used for more advanced diving

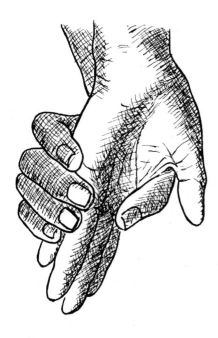

Figure 15.2 Hand clasp for entry.

- for a safe entry the arms should be extended beyond the head with the hands firmly clasped together (Fig. 15.2)
- encourage a good standard of performance. Keeping the interest of the pupils through help and praise will help discipline, safety and enjoyment.

Starting to dive

The initial stages in diving are introduced alongside early swimming practices and are combined in a watermanship programme. Throughout the learning process the pupils should know why they are performing certain tasks, what they are trying to achieve and, within safety limits, they should be encouraged to experiment and to progress at their own rate. The teacher/coach should monitor carefully the progress being made by each pupil, particularly checking that one stage is confidently performed before moving on. The more adventurous and able pupil may dive easily, requiring few lead-up stages, whilst the more timid pupil will need constant help at each stage and should not be forced on to the poolside before confidence has been gained through activities practised in the water.

Early practices in the water

Many of the practices in Chapter 10, shown under rotation and orientation, submersion, regaining the surface and flotation shapes, can be utilised as early water activities in relation to diving. These basic practices are essential to give confidence and enjoyment and they should be fully mastered before proceeding to the poolside. Water practices are designed to develop:

- confidence in being under water with the eyes open
- breath control
- familiarity with the inverted position
- an awareness of body line and body tension
- the ability to rotate the body
- vertical thrust through the legs
- the ability to resurface

The practices given are only a selection and can be supplemented by the teacher/coach. Practices should be selected according to the needs of the class and of individual pupils. In any class pupils may be working at different activities at the same time.

Submerging and surfacing practices

Initially in shallow water, although some may be repeated out of the swimmer's depth as confidence increases. In all these activities the eyes should be open underwater and goggles should not be worn.

137

Task	**Teaching/coaching points and progression**
1 Basic introductory work concerned with 'face into the water' (See Chapter 10).	Eyes open. Let the water run off the face do not wipe it. Blow bubbles in the water.
2 Which part of the body can touch the pool floor? (seat, knees, hand, back, hip, elbows, front).	How do they submerge? Limit breath intake. Hands using sculling actions to direct the body and hold a submerged position.
3 Move underwater in a variety of ways. Going round, through or under apparatus at various depths. Retrieving objects from the pool floor.	Head and shoulders low, hips high, to submerge. Eyes open when working. Move underwater in a variety of ways. Progress these activities to deeper water.
4 Push from the pool wall and glide to the pool floor, touch the pool floor with hands then feet to push back to the surface.	Hips high to push from the side. Arms and body stretched. Head down between the arms. Body curled to transfer weight from hands to feet ready for a strong push up to resurface.
	Progress gradually to deeper water until this can be performed in the diving area of the pool.
5 Submerge to sit on the pool floor, then feet on the pool floor, push back to the surface.	Spring up, lift arms high to aid submerging. Exhale gradually blowing bubbles. Scull with palms facing upwards to stay down. Eyes open. Strong push up from feet flat on pool floor.
6 Porpoise dives through hoops on the surface of the water.	Strong push from the pool floor to lift hips high. Head down between arms. Continue dive until hands then feet touch the pool floor, push up to resurface.

Practices for awareness of body line, tension and rotation

Tasks	**Teaching/coaching points**
1 Pushing and gliding on the front, the back, the side and with rotation.	Knees bent at the pool wall to give a strong push away. Long, thin body shape. Hands clasped one on top of the other, head between the arms.
2 Changing positions during glide.	Example: tight tuck position, arms encircling lower legs. (See Mushroom Float position, Fig. 10.15, page 101).
3 Rotating movements around horizontal and vertical axis.	Encourage experimental approach. How is rotation initiated? Use of sculling hand actions.
4 Pushing and gliding into a somersault on the front and on the back.	Tension in each body position. Feet close to seat on somersault. Awareness of body position throughout.
5 Handstands taken from pushing and gliding. Holding the handstand position with the legs straight and together. Bringing the feet to the pool floor to a tucked body position ready for recovery.	Strong bend at the hips to initiate the rotation, head down, pull down with the arms. Encourage a straight leg lift, tension in the held position. Handstand controlled by the head position.

6 Gliding on the back, rotating backwards into a handstand. Tuck and push up to return to the surface.	Head back, shoulder extension, strong leg lift, tension in body and legs. Feet to pool floor for strong push up.

Activities to develop springing and the inverted position – shallow water

The main purpose of this group of activities is to encourage the pupils to use their legs to gain maximum height and to develop a spring into the inverted position.

Tasks	Teaching/coaching points
Practices from standing in shallow water – waist to shoulder depth	
1 Springing high, repeat the springing action several times.	Bend knees, push hard through the legs and hips. Let the legs give to absorb the landing and be ready to push up again.
2 Springing high to show a fully stretched streamlined position.	Hands clasped together, head between the arms, body stretched.
3 Springing high to show different body shapes. Match a partner's movement.	Shape to be shown clearly. Suggest – wide, thin, tucked or asymmetrical.
4 Springing up to a straight shape with rotation around a longitudinal axis.	Use head and bring one arm across the body to initiate the turn. Keep the body streamlined. Spring high.
5 Springing high and attempting to bring the shoulders to meet the water first on descent.	High spring, bring hips up, twist or rotate to bring the shoulders down. This is a free tumbling activity to develop confidence and body awareness.
6 Springing high and trying to place the hands on the pool floor. This is a crouch jump with knees bent.	Lift hips up, heels to seat, hands to replace feet. Head down, eyes open.
7 Springing into a somersault using either a forward or backward take off.	Arms in a "Y" position to start. Spring hips up. Tuck the body tightly, eyes open. Finish in a standing position.
8 Working with a partner. Springing over or through apparatus (hoop, stick, float). Different body parts leading from forward, backward and sideways take-off.	Encourage free work. Spring into handstands, somersaults or shallow glide. Eyes open, lift hips. Use the arms to help the lift.
9 Taking a spring dive movement from a stance in the water with the arms in a "Y" shape. Spring into a handstand or take a shallower oblique entry into a glide.	Spring high. Bring hands together with the head between them. Awareness of legs together, body stretched on glide or handstand.

These early practices may be introduced as contrasting activities in swimming lessons. They should be repeated to give ample time for the pupils to become really confident underwater and able to control their bodies and develop good thrust. Practices should be selected to suit individual abilities and, before moving on to the next stage, all pupils should be confident when out of their depth, and able to perform a handstand with ease and control in the shallow water.

139

Surface Dive in deep water (Water depth 1.5-2.0 metres minimum)

Task	Teaching/coaching points
1 From the pool wall pushing into a glide underwater, and continuing the glide to the surface.	Feet high on the wall to give a strong push. Head tightly between the arms, good streamlined body shape. Push about 0.5-1.0 metre under the water, hold the glide. Continue the glide on the water surface.
2 Pushing from the wall into a glide into a head first Surface Dive. Returning to the surface by taking the feet to the pool floor for a strong push up.	Strong bend at the hips into a shape. Strong downward pull with the arms followed by a sweep with the palms leading to an extended position above the head.
3 Surface Dive to recover a weighted object or series of objects. This practice ensures the eyes are open when under the water.	Head pressed down. Straight leg lift to give an inverted, vertical, streamlined body shape. Return to the surface from a strong push from the pool floor.

Poolside activities (Water depth 1.8 metres minimum)
Feet first entries

Tasks	Teaching/coaching points
1 Stepping to enter the water in a stretched position.	Toes over the edge. Small step forward. Body straight for entry, arms by the side of the body. Let the body completely submerge before pushing or kicking to the surface.
2 Springing from two feet to show clear body shapes in flight:	Toes gripping the pool edge. Push hard through the feet and swing the arms to initiate a high spring.
(i) Long and thin, hands stretched above the head in the flight with the hands clasped (Fig. 15.3).	Head held in alignment with the spine, eyes looking slightly upwards. On take-off the arms lift forwards and upwards reaching high. After the peak of the jump the arms sweep sideways and downwards to the thighs for the streamlined entry.
(ii) Tucked position on the flight (Fig. 15.4).	Body extended on take-off as above. Then knees brought up to the chest with the hands gripping the lower legs. The head must be kept up with the eyes looking forwards. Shoot the feet downwards for a vertical entry as in stretched jump above.
(iii) High spring into a twist. Twisting to both left and right.	Pupils to find out what helps them to twist, relating to the earlier work in shallow water. Swing the arm across the body in the direction of the twist. Body kept straight, head in line but turning in the direction of the twist.

Figure 15.3 Flight – stretched shape.   *Figure 15.4 Flight – tucked shape.*

Safety

These jumps should always be taken from a standing take-off into water of adequate depth related to the height and weight of the swimmer. There must be clear signals given for entry and return to the side. (See page 135). Pupils who can now perform a Surface Dive in deep water, and are able to jump in from the poolside, should be ready to progress to diving from the poolside. Many pupils who have mastered these skills will have the confidence to go straight into a Plunge Dive and may not require any further leading-up stages.

141

Figure 15.5 Standing position.

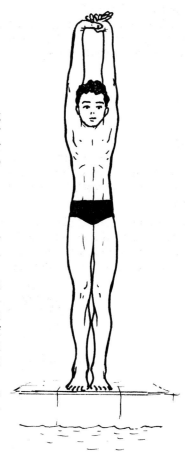

Head first entries

Some pupils may need further guided practices before attempting the Plunge Dive because they are still fearful of entering the water head first from the poolside. When selecting starting positions for diving practices it is preferable to use those from which it is easy to over balance.

Safety reminders

- check the depth of the water for all levels of divers from any starting position. Entries by the inexperienced are unpredictable
- remind pupils to clasp their hands together when stretched above the head and to feel that their upper arms are squeezing their ears. Standing on the poolside in a fully stretched position with the arms above the head gives the feeling of tension throughout the body, and the squeezing of the head between the arms. In this position the palm of one hand grasps the back of the other hand in a squeeze grip (Fig. 15.5). Remind pupils to check their free water space before diving and ensure they understand the entry and exit organisation. (See page 135).

Starting positions	Teaching/coaching points
1 Crouch position (Fig. 15.6) Crouching on the poolside with the feet together and the knees apart, the toes gripping the edge. The arms are extended above the head with the hands clasped together.	Bend forward, keeping the head between the arms, overbalance and stretch towards the water. It is a roll into the water with a hip lift to go into the extension. The chin should be on the chest.
2 Astride position Standing on the poolside with the feet comfortably apart and the toes gripping the pool edge. Let the knees bend. The body is bent forwards with the head between the arms and the hands clasped together.	Bend forward until the hands nearly touch the water. Transfer the weight forward and the body should slide into the water. Encourage less bend at the hips as confidence increases.

142

3 **Lunge position** (Fig. 15.7)
One foot is placed at the edge of the pool with toes gripping the edge. The other foot is stretched behind with the toes just touching the floor.

The body is inclined forwards as the back leg lifts like a see-saw. The body overbalances, the lift of the rear leg controls the overbalance and gives a good body line. As the hands reach the water the front leg joins the other leg to give a good entry position. The head must be kept between the arms and the speed of the leg lift controlled. It is a fall into the water.

4 **Pike Fall** (Fig. 15.8)
Stand on the poolside with the feet together and the toes gripping the edge. Bend at the waist into a tight pike position with the head in line with the body.

Transfer the weight forward and let the body topple into the water. Keep the legs straight throughout. As the body topples forwards and outwards, straighten out for a streamlined entry.

The above practices are based on a fall into the water by moving the centre of gravity in front of the feet. They encourage a head first entry and a stretched body position from an easy overbalance. Divers should now be ready to incorporate a spring into the movement. It may help to revise some of the head first springing practices in shallow water. Practise the hip lift and the push through the feet.

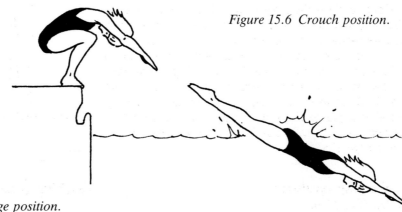

Figure 15.6 Crouch position.

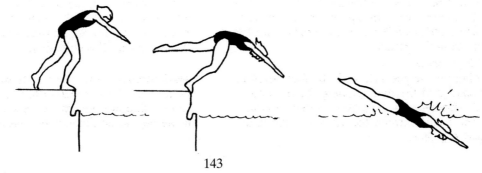

Figure 15.7 Lunge position.

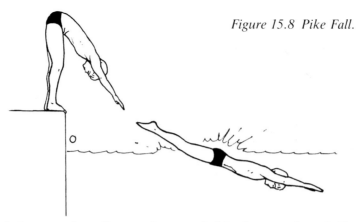

Figure 15.8 Pike Fall.

Practices requiring spring from the poolside into a head first entry

As the following practices are to lead to a Plunge Dive the angle of entry will be 14°-20° to the water. This is also necessary for safety purposes where the water is only 1.8 metres in depth. Use the four starting positions already described for the dive falls but incorporate a strong push from the feet as the body begins to overbalance. Many pupils will go straight to the Plunge Dive and not require the following stages.

Starting positions	Teaching/coaching points
1 **Semi-crouch position** Feet astride or together.	As the body over balances push from the feet and lift the hips. Head kept between the arms, stretch for the entry.
2 **Lunge position** (Fig. 15.7) As this is a one foot take-off ensure that the toes grip the pool edge.	Push from the front foot as the rear leg lifts and the body tips forwards. Encourage a stretch out for the entry.
3 **High Crouch dive** (Fig. 15.9) Feet together on the poolside, hands above the head. Lean forwards but only a little way.	Push vigorously through the feet and hips as the body tips forwards. Extend to the entry. Keep the head between the arms but look to the entry point.
4 **Spring Header** (Fig. 15.10) N.B. Check water depth. Stand on the poolside with the feet together, toes gripping the edge. The arms taking a "Y" position. There is a slight lean forward from the hips bringing the shoulders in front of the hips. The knees are bent slightly.	Keep the head in line with the trunk. Focus the eyes forwards to the entry point. Drive vigorously up from the feet through the hips to follow a curved pathway in flight. During the flight close the arms to the stretched position. The body should be stretched to a streamline entry with head in, hands clasped, legs together and stretched.

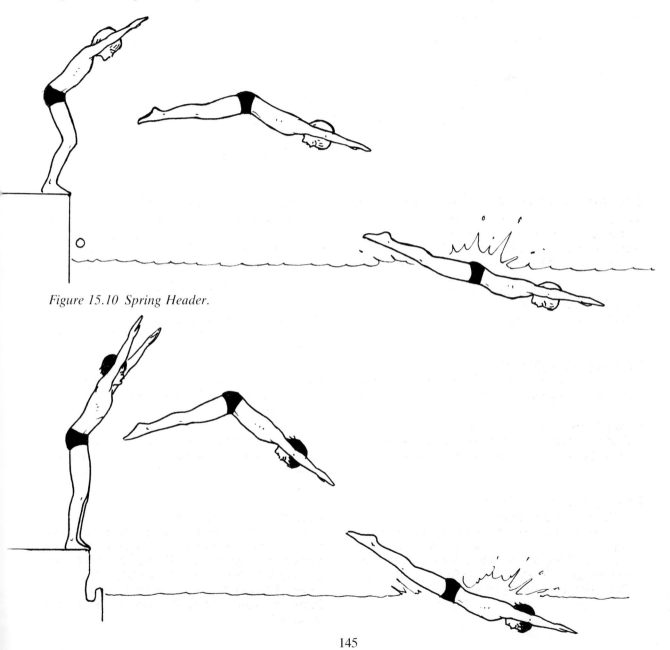

Figure 15.9 High Crouch position.

Figure 15.10 Spring Header.

Additional practices

These practices should be executed in a minimum of 1.8 metres.

Sitting Dive – introduction

Providing the early confidence practices have been mastered, including a Surface Dive, it is not generally necessary to use a Sitting Dive. But some pupils, particularly adults, find this a comfortable and stable starting position. However, the design of the pool might make the starting position difficult to achieve. For a head first entry it is necessary to lift the body weight from the very stable sitting position; some people achieve this by standing on the trough or rail, which may present a slippery base. It is very difficult to perform in a deck level pool where an astride standing position is preferable.

Sitting Dive – description (Fig. 15.11)

The pupils sit on the edge of the pool with their feet resting on the rail or trough. The feet and knees may be together or slightly apart. The arms are raised above the head with the hands gripped tightly. The pupil bends forward and raises the hips to over-balance into the water. The feet should remain in contact with the rail until the body is submerging. It is a roll into the water.

Kneeling Dive (Fig. 15.12)

The same roll into the water may be taken from a kneeling starting position. Many people find this an uncomfortable starting position, particularly where the poolside is rough. A Lunge Dive is probably a more comfortable option. A kneeling position is taken up with one knee close to the pool edge and the toes of the front foot girmly gripping the edge. The toes of the rear foot are curled under to give a base from which to push. With the arms stretched above the head the body rolls forwards to touch the forward knee. As the body overbalances there is a push from the feet and the body stretches out into a glide position underwater.

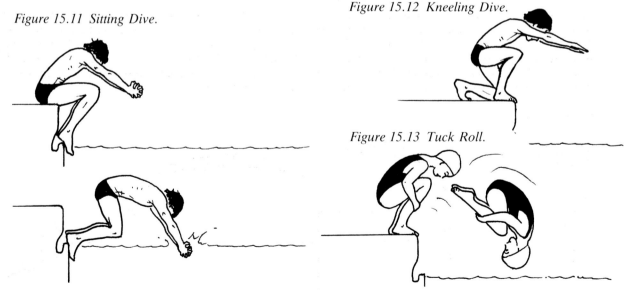

Figure 15.11 Sitting Dive.

Figure 15.12 Kneeling Dive.

Figure 15.13 Tuck Roll.

Tuck Roll (Fig. 15.13)

This is an activity enjoyed by pupils who can already accomplish a forward roll from standing in the shallow end and is an early leading up stage to somersaults from the poolside. It is usually a progression used in diving and may cause pupils to continue to somersault on entry instead of adopting a stretched position. The pupils crouch on the poolside in a tight tuck position with the body as compact as possible. The head is tucked in and the hands hold the shins. The weight transfers forward to initiate a roll into the water, the body is kept in the tight tuck throughout the movement. The head must be kept in.

The Plunge Dive (Fig. 15.14)

This dive is similar to a Racing Dive required as a start for any prone stroke and it is a useful shallow dive entry for recreational swimmers. When learning this dive it should be performed into at least 1.8 metres of water.

Stance – the feet are placed approximately hip width apart with the toes curled over the edge to give a good grip. The knees are bent to give stability and to prepare for the spring. The back is curved with the neck following the curve of the back and the chin lowered slightly to the chest. The eyes look towards the point of entry. The arms hang down loosely from the shoulders. The diver should feel balanced and relaxed.

Take off – the body weight is transferred forward by action/reaction as the arms swing back slightly. As the body overbalances the arms swing forwards strongly giving impetus to the forward movement. There is a vigorous thrust from the feet and legs and extension of the hips, knees, ankles and toes. The feet drive back against the poolside to give forward and upward momentum.

Flight – after an initial hip lift to give some height to the dive the body extends to a streamlined position. The arms are fully extended beyond the head, which is squeezed between the arms, and is in line with the body. The hands should be clasped together. The line of flight is upwards and outwards. There should be a feeling of stretch from the finger tips to the pointed toes.

Entry – a shallow clean entry should be made, the hands lead into the water followed by the whole body which remains in the extended position until completely submerged. The hands must remain together for the entry, the head between the arms, the legs and feet together and stretched. There should not be any slapping of the water. The streamlined glide should be held after the entry. The resurfacing should not be rushed as this can cause a sudden hollowing of the back which may give pain and strain. Full advantage should be taken of the glide to move smoothly into a swimming stroke.

Figure 15.14 Plunge Dive.

147

Faults, possible causes and some examples of corrective measures

Many faults in diving arise from lack of confidence. This usually implies that the diver has progressed too quickly to the poolside and needs time to work at shallow water practices, surface dives and jumps. Faults during flight or entry can in most cases be traced to an incorrect take-off. The flight of the dive is determined by the power and angle of the take-off.

Fault	Cause	Correction
An unbalanced stance	Standing on the toes. Toes not gripping pool, etc. No firm knee bend. A poor stance may indicate a lack of confidence.	Check the position of the whole body particularly feet and legs. If there appears a lack of confidence return to jump practices and submerging practices.
Lack of power in the take-off	Falling too far forwards before thrusting. Lack of push against the poolside. Not using the arm swing or mistiming the arm swing. No smooth bend and stretch in the ankles and knees.	Practise jumps emphasising the knee bend and push up through the legs. Emphasise the strong arm swing aiming for a distant entry. Work at the co-ordination of the thrust from the legs and the arm swing. Set a point for them to aim for on entry.
Lack of height in the initial flight	Falling too far forwards. Aiming down rather than up and out. Lack of leg thrust. Lack of hip lift as the body leaves the poolside.	Take jumping practices working on the take-off. Return to the Spring Header to help thrust and lift. Explain that height is necessary to give distance in flight.
Lack of body tension in flight	Poor body awareness. Some anxiety about the new skill.	Return to practices for body stretch, particularly standing on the poolside and reaching up high. Take gliding practices. Remind the pupils to feel a firm stretch throughout the body.
Flat entry	Falling into the water. Lifting the head. Lack of spring. Lack of confidence.	Return to earlier submerging and gliding practices. Use jumps and Spring Header practices to help the take-off. Remind the pupils of correct head position throughout.
Hands apart on entry	Lack of confidence to stretch for the entry.	Standing on the side with the hands clasped together above the head. Gliding, jumping and earlier dives checking hands clasped and the arms pressed against the ears.
Slapping the water on entry	Thinking it will prevent sinking. Trying to go too quickly into a stroke. Too shallow an entry.	Emphasize the lift on take-off and streamlined entry without splash and with the head between the arms.
Surfacing too quickly	Lifting the head and hands quickly after entry.	Stress retaining the underwater glide. Try to hold the glide across the pool or to a particular pool floor line. Practise in the water push glide and hold the glide.

Having progressed to the Plunge Dive pupils have a safe way of entering the water head first. It is a dive which may be used in a survival or lifesaving situation and with further teaching/coaching can be adapted to a Racing Dive.

Figure 15.15 Plain Header.

The Plain Header – introduction

Some pupils may wish to learn a Plain Header dive from the poolside as it is the basic dive to be mastered before going on to springboard and highboard diving. This dive requires a vertical entry which must only be performed into deep water, **the minimum depth is the height of the diver with the arms extended fully above their head plus 0.5 metre.**

The Plain Header – description (Fig. 15.15)

This is very similar to the Spring Header but it commences from an upright position with the arms in a "Y" position and the eyes looking ahead. Ensure that there is a safe, adequate depth of water.

Teaching/coaching points

Stance – toes gripping the pool edge. Pelvis tucked under and the stomach firm. Whole body, whilst not tense, must be firm. Head in line with the body. Arms slightly more than shoulder width apart. Palms facing forwards with the fingers together.

Take-off – smooth knee band. Strong push up through the ankles and toes as the knees straighten. Contract the stomach to lift the hips to a slight pike position. Body remains firm with the arms in "Y" position.

Flight – there is minimum of body movement. Legs fully stretched with feet together and pointed. The hands are clasped together prior to entry. The eyes spot the entry point.

Entry – clean entry. Body fully extended. Head between the arms. Entry near to vertical but not beyond. Dive taken to the pool bottom.

Recovery – place feet flat on pool bottom. Push hard to the surface of the water.

Motivation

Chapter 1 makes reference to the need to motivate pupils. The ASA Diving Awards are a good example of motivating the mastery of preliminary diving skills.

Progression

Having achieved a good Plunge Dive or Plain Header pupils may wish to progress to board diving. By joining a diving club where there are good facilities it is possible to progress safely, to enjoy the sport and the companionship. Membership of a club can open up a whole range of competitive opportunities.

End Piece to Part IV
Other general swimming activities

Introduction
In addition to the four main strokes already described there are others that are no longer used in competition. They are well worth learning for recreational purposes or for their adaptation and application to other activities in water.

Elementary Backstroke
Body position
The body lies on the back in an almost horizontal position with the face clear of the water. With the head raised a little or with the eyes looking towards the feet, a lower leg position will result, so that the knees are not likely to break the water surface on recovery. The increased resistance caused by this position presents no problem because speed is unimportant.

Leg action
The purpose of the leg kick is to provide propulsion and to maintain the desired body position. The pathway of the action is similar to that of an inverted Breaststroke, and the emphasis should be on flexed ankles so that the kick is felt to be made with the soles of the feet

- **recovery** – in this action the knees are bent by dropping the lower legs with heels moving towards the seat. The heels should be hip width or more apart, ready for the drive backwards. The thighs remain almost in line with the body just under the surface of the water. The position of the knees is relatively unimportant although the distance between tends to be narrow rather than wide. A wide action of the feet will cause some flexion of the hips and the body to be more inclined to the surface.
- **propulsion** – with the heels well apart and the ankles flexed, the drive is slightly outward and backward. The feet move through a circular pathway and the inside borders, as well as the sides of the feet, push against the water to gain propulsion. The legs may or may not move together depending on the activity for which the stroke is intended.

Arm action
This might be described as a wide sculling action

- **recovery** – the hands are moved simultaneously under water, being pulled upwards, close to the body, from thighs to chest, then swept sideways until the arms are extended and almost in line with the shoulders, in preparation for the propulsive action
- **propulsion** – with the palms of the hands gaining purchase on the water, the extended arms are pressed strongly backwards and inwards, towards the sides of the body.

Breathing
No problems are presented because the face is clear of the water throughout the stroke. Normally, breath would be taken on recovery and exhaled with propulsion.

Timing of the stroke (co-ordination)
This is fairly simple. Leg movements tend to precede arm actions but they appear to be simultaneous. There is no pause between the end of recovery and the beginning of propulsion. A glide may be held with the body in an extended position, at the end of the propulsive actions (Fig. IV.1).

(Old) English Backstroke
This is a development of the Elementary Backstroke performed with an identical leg action, already described, but using a double over arm action.

Body position and leg action
As for Elementary Backstroke.

Arm action
- **recovery** – from a position at the sides of the body the arms are lifted from the water, simultaneously, and then carried to an extended position in advance of the head. They enter the water, slightly wider than the shoulders, dependent mainly on the flexibility of the shoulder girdle. When the hands are about 15cms below the surface the pull begins after a smooth transition from the entry.
- **propulsion** – with the arms remaining straight, the hands follow semi-circular pathways. They are at their deepest in the water as they pass the shoulders when the pull changes to a push. This continues until the hands reach the hips, with the arms at the sides of the body.

Breathing
Normally, inhalation takes place as the arms swing overhead, during which action there is a slight raising of the head and upper body. Exhalation takes place during propulsion.

Timing of the stroke (co-ordination)
The recovery of the arms coincides with the propulsive action of the legs, at the end of which movement the body is fully extended with the arms overhead. The legs remain close together during the powerful pull-push action of the arms.

Sidestroke
Body Position
As the name suggests, the swimmer lies in the water, on either side, as streamlined and horizontal as possible. The side of the head is in the water with the eyes and nose just above the surface.

Leg action
From an extended position, and moving simultaneously, the legs with one above the other, begin their recovery. The upper leg moves forward and the lower leg moves backward with the knees bending and the heels moving towards the seat. Propulsion occurs as the legs are swept together through a circular pathway, back to the extended position which is held during a glide. The action is sometimes called a 'scissor' kick.

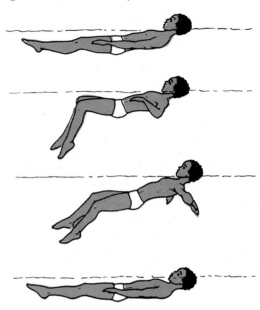

Figure IV.1 Elementary Backstroke.

Arm action

During the glide the upper arm lies along the upper side of the body, with the lower arm extended forwards in advance of the head. From these positions the arms move simultaneously. The upper arm recovers as it moves forwards to a position with elbow bent and the hand below the head. At the same time the lower arm is propelling as it pulls in a downward-sideways direction to meet the other arm, in a similar position, with elbow bent and the hand below the head. Still moving simultaneously, and without pausing, the arms are now extended with the upper arm propelling as it pushes downwards-backwards, while the lower arm recovers, as it extends to the forward position.

Breathing

Inhalation normally takes place during the propulsive action of the lower arm which tends to raise the upper body and head and as the glide begins, exhalation takes place through nose and mouth.

Timing of the stroke (co-ordination)

From the extended position, while the arms are moving inward to their bent positions, the legs recover to their bent positions ready for the propulsive kick, which is accompanied by the extension of the arms. Then follows a short glide before the actions are repeated (Fig. IV.2).

Variations

This stroke may also be performed as follows:
– with an out of water recovery of the upper arm using an action similar to that of the Front Crawl Stroke,
– with each arm recovering over the water with the body rolling alternately to the side of the pulling arm, and with each leg in turn being uppermost during the kick. It was from this latter form that the Front Crawl stroke was originally developed.

Surface Diving

There are two methods of Surface Diving. The head first dive is best known, but equally effective, and easier to perform, is the feet first method of submerging:

● Head First Dive

The swimmer moves in the prone position, performs a strong Breaststroke arm pull which is continued towards the sides of the body. During the pull the head and shoulders are thrust forcibly downward whilst the body bends sharply at the hips. As the body rotates the

Figure IV.2 Sidestroke.

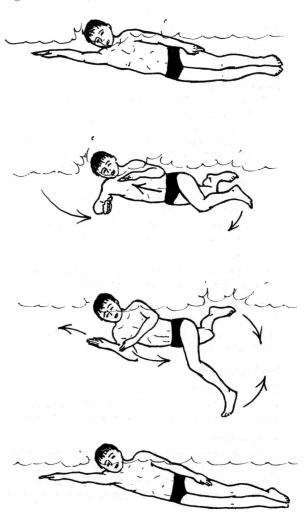

153

Figure IV.3 Head First Surface Dive.

arms are swept forward underwater and the legs are raised upward to a vertical position. The whole body now in line, submerges under its own weight. It is important that the swimmer should have the confidence and ability to remain in the vertical position for some time, to allow the weight of the legs to assist the descent (Fig. IV.3). As the dive requires the body to be rotated until it is inverted, skills such as handstanding in shallow water and somersaulting are useful preparatory activities which will also help to establish confidence agility and control of breathing.

● Feet First Dive

The Feet First Dive is performed by making a powerful downward Breaststroke type kick together with a vigorous downward thrust with the hands, thus raising the upper part of the body as high as possible from the water. With maximum body weight above the surface, with the legs brought together and the arms held at the sides, the streamlined, vertical body will sink below the surface (Fig. IV.4). If greater depth is required before swimming begins, the hands can be pressed upwards towards the surface, so forcing the body deeper in the water. Alternatively, in performing the dive, the arms can be raised above the head following the leg kick, thereby adding to the unsupported weight of the upper body and assisting the sinking process. This method has advantages for swimmers with a weak kick who find difficulty in forcing the upper part of the body above the water surface. However, it has the disadvantage that it makes the transfer to the swimming position more difficult to achieve.

In both types of Feet First Dive it is essential that the body remains in the vertical position during the sinking movement. The swimming position underwater is achieved by tucking the body and rotating forwards through 90 degrees. When the rotation is completed the body is extended into the prone swimming position.

154

Figure IV.4 Feet First Surface Dive.

Underwater swimming

After the Surface Dive, the logical progression is the underwater swim. Methods of achieving propulsion are:

– using a Breaststroke leg action with the arms pulling around to the sides of the body
– using the same arm action with a Front Crawl type kick
– using a Front Paddle action with the arms and a Front Crawl kick

PART V

ADDITIONAL INFORMATION

FURTHER READING

ASA, *ASA Handbook*, ASA (Annual publication)

Austin G., Noble J., *Swimming for Fitness*, A & C Black (1990)

British Association of National Coaches (BANC), *The Growing Child in Competitive Sport*, BANC International Congress Proceedings (1987)

British Institute of Sports Coaches (formerly BANC) International Congress Proceedings (1989)

Counsilman J., *The Science of Swimming*, Pelham Books (1968)

Counsilman J., *Competitive Swimming Manual for Coaches and Swimmers*, Pelham Books (1978)

Cregeen A. et al, (Edit.) *Babes in the Water*, ASA/Savlon (1984)

Cregeen A. et al, (Edit.) *The Teaching of Swimming*, 15th revised edition, ASA (1989)

Cregeen A., MacKenzie-Farmer A., (Edit.) *Water Activities for Parent and Babies*, ASA (1989)

Cross R., (Edit.) *The ASA Guide to Better Swimming*, Pan Books (1987)

Cross R., *How to Coach Swimming*, Collins (1990)

Donlan A., *Survival in Cold Water – a handbook for teachers*, ASA (1989)

Eaton D., (Edit.) *Life Saving*, Royal Life Saving Society (1990)

Elkington H. & Chamberlain J., *Synchronised Swimming*, David & Charles (1986)

Gleeson G., (Edit.) *The Growing Child in Competitive Sport*, Hodder & Stoughton and British Association of National Coaches (1986)

Glover M., *Water Polo Coaching Manual*, National Water Polo Coaches Association (1985), 117 Urmston Lane, Stretford, Manchester, M32 9DE

Gray J., *Diving Instruction*, ASA (1978)

Hardy C., *Handbook for the Teacher of Swimming*, Pelham (1987)

Hardy C., *Let's Go Swimming*, Stanley Thornes (1989)

Harrison J., (Edit.) *Teaching of Swimming for those with Special Needs*, ASA (1986)

Harrison J., *Anyone Can Swim*, The Crowood Press, (1989)

Institute of Baths & Recreation Management, *Diving into Swimming Pools*, IBRM (1990)

Knapp B., *Skill in Sport – the attainment of proficiency*, Routledge & Kegan Paul (1963)

Maglischo E., *Swimming Faster*, Mayfield Publishing Co (1982)

National Coaching Foundation, *Introductory Study Packs 1-7*, NCF (1984)

National Coaching Foundation, *Coaching Handbooks 1-3*, NCF (1986)

Sports Council, *Safety in Swimming Pools*, Sports Council/Health & Safety Commission (1988)

Verrier J., *Swimming*, The Crowood Press (1988)

Wellington P. & Cross C., *Nutrition for Swimming – your personal guide*, National Coaching Foundation (1990)

Wilke K., Madsen Ø., *Coaching the Young Swimmer*, Pelham Books (1986)

Wootton S., *Nutrition for Sport*, Simon & Schuster (1989)

Journals

Swimming Times, published monthly by *Swimming Times Ltd*, Address as for ASA.

Coaching Focus, published three times a year by *NCF* (See address list).

ADDRESSES

The Amateur Swimming
  Association,
Harold Fern House,
Derby Square,
Loughborough,
Leicestershire LE11 0AL
Telephone: 01509 230431

Institute of Swimming Teachers
  and Coaches,
Dawson House,
63 Forest Road,
Loughborough,
Leicestershire LE11 3NW
Telephone: 01509 264357

Royal Life Saving Society UK,
Mountbatten House,
Studley,
Warwickshire B80 7NN
Telephone: 0152 785 3943

Ireland & Northern Ireland
The Irish ASA,
The House of Sport,
Long Mile Road,
Dublin 12

Scotland
The Scottish ASA,
Holmhills Farm,
Greenlees Road,
Cambuslang,
Glasgow G72 8TD

Wales
The Welsh ASA,
Wales Empire Pool,
Wood Street,
Cardiff CF1 1PP

Australia
Australian Swimming Inc.,
PO Box 169,
Kippax,
ACT 2615,
Australia

RLSS Australia,
PO Box 1567
North Sydney,
New South Wales 2059,
Australia

Canada
Canadian ASA,
16 James Naismith Drive,
Gloucester,
Ontario,
Canada K1B 5N4

RLSS Canada,
191 Church Street,
Toronto,
Canada M5B 1Y7

India
Swimming Federation of India,
27 Paraskunj Society 1,
Setallite Road,
Ahmedabad 380 015,
India

New Zealand
New Zealand ASA,
PO Box 11-115,
Wellington,
New Zealand

RLSS New Zealand,
264 Armagh Street,
PO Box 13-489,
Christchurch,
New Zealand

FINA, Av. de Beaumont 9,
Rez-de-chausse,
1012 Lausanne,
Switzerland

National Coaching Foundation,
114 Cardigan Road,
Headingley,
Leeds,
LS6 3BJ

British Institute of Sports
  Coaches, (formerly BANC),
2 College Close,
Beckett Park,
Leeds
LS6 3QH
Telephone: 0113 2753365

The Sports Council,
16 Upper Woburn Place,
London
WC1H 0QP

Institute of Sport & Recreation
  Management
Gifford House,
36/38 Sherrard Street,
Melton Mowbray,
Leicestershire
LE13 1XJ

Health and Safety Executive,
Baynards House,
1 Chepstow Place,
Westbourne Grove,
London
W2 4TF

THE ASA AWARDS SCHEME

As the National Governing Body of the sport the ASA's responsibilities range from Parent and Child water activities up to major competitions, as well as taking in the promotion of healthy recreational swimming for all. The key feature of those responsibilities is the training of teachers/coaches. The *ASA Awards Scheme* contributes to the fulfilment of those responsibilities by offering a wide range of activities catering for all ages and abilities. It is designed to reflect a good educational base with a logical progression from earliest stages to specialist disciplines.

Note

Teachers/coaches and tutors should note that the following is only an outline of the complete **ASA Awards Scheme,** and should ensure they provide complete and accurate information to their pupils.

Rainbow Awards

These are distance awards, recommended for children of 5 years and upwards, with tests from 5 metres to 5000 metres. There are no time limits or set styles. The swims should be completed without pausing and without stress to the swimmer.

Water Skills

These consist of six progressive grades. The first three of these are particularly valuable for the early swimmer and those with disabilities, whilst the latter grades wet the appetite for water polo, synchronised swimming and diving.

National Challenge

Again, six grades which test abilities in stroke technique as well as being able to swim further.

Personal Survival

This takes into account the latest research into immersion in cold water and is designed to test both the swimmers' ability in survival techniques as well as the knowledge of why given actions are taken.

Speed Swimming

This intended to introduce swimmers to the competitive scene and the early awards are aimed at the average child over short distances on the four major strokes. The Merit and Advanced grades, naturally, test the abilities even further and faster.

Preliminary Diving Skills

These reflect the safety implications before learning to dive, and they lead the novice towards becoming a skilled and safe diver.

Water Polo

These awards introduce the basic ball handling skills of the game, both moving and static.

Synchronised Swimming

The Preliminary award has the attractions of both the artistic and gymnastic challenges, whilst the latter five grades become much more specialised.

The Ultimate Swimmer

This tests a wide range of skills in all disciplines. When four named compulsory awards, plus four optional awards chosen by the swimmer, have been completed and recorded in an official log book, which is then sent to the ASA, the achievement is recognised by the awarding of a free costume badge and scroll.

Swim Fit

This award is designed primarily for adults by motivating them into setting themselves achievement targets within a swimming programme. If used regularly it can contribute to the health and fitness of the non-competitor, or be used in conjunction with a competitor's training regime. There are a wide range of distances available.

Certificate of Merit

This is a special certificate presented to people who have been successful in gaining an award under adverse conditions.

For people with Special Needs

In line with modern educational trends the ASA has made several of its main stream awards available to swimmers with a special need.

General Information

- **Spiral Bound Handbook**

  The schemes are all published in one book which makes it easy for the teacher to compare and choose the skills on offer. Pupils can also see the colourful badges available to mark their achievements.

- **Awards Log Book**

  This enables swimmers to see at a glance their next award, and helps them to remain motivated to progress through the various schemes.

- **Blank Certificates**

  These are very popular. They are open-ended certificates which can be used to record achievements or provide incentives for everyone, from babies to Senior Citizens. They are also a means of rewarding those whose disabilities might prevent them from attaining the more formal targets, but nevertheless deserve recognition for their efforts.

Information covering the whole of the ASA Awards Scheme may be obtained from the ASA, Harold Fern House, Derby Square, Loughborough, Leicestershire, LE11 0AL.

NOTES ON CONTRIBUTING AUTHORS

Anne Cradock

Anne qualified as a teacher of Physical Education at Ansty College of Physical Education. Later became a Physical Education Adviser for the City of Birmingham and, after a period away whilst having a family, is now an Advisory Teacher in Physical Education (Swimming) for Birmingham Education Department. Anne is an ASA Principal Tutor, an Advanced Teacher (Swimming), Teacher (Disabled), Teacher (Synchro), as well as being an RLSS Distinction holder and a Grade I RLSS Examiner. Anne serves on several ASA committees and working parties associated with the development of education and training of teachers/coaches in the sport.

Cliff Dedynski

Cliff is an ASA Coach and currently Chief Coach to the Oundle and District Swim Squad. His successes include placing swimmers in national teams for the last 5 years or so, whilst the Oundle men's team has made the finals of the GB Championship for the last 3 years. He is currently a member of the ASA Publications and Visual Aids Working Party and was previously a member of the ASA Coach Committee. Outside of swimming, Cliff is a Senior Lecturer in management, business and legal studies at Nene College, Northampton.

Alan Donlan

Before becoming Honorary Secretary of the ASA Education Committee in 1973, a post he still holds, Alan was District Education Secretary for the North Eastern Counties ASA. He is also a Director of *Swimming Times* Ltd and a member of the Joint ASA/ISTC Working Party reviewing ASA qualifications in preparation for the introduction of National Vocational Qualifications. Alan has contributed to several books and papers on various aspects of swimming education. He is a former competitive swimmer and water polo player and also used to teach/coach one of the oldest swimming clubs in the NE District. Outside of swimming he is Principal Assistant Secretary with a GCSE examining group.

Bill Furniss

Bill has coached professionally for 16 years. He has coached both junior and senior internationals, the NOVA Centurion Swimming Club and the Nottingham City Council Swim Squad, one of the country's leading swim squads. Bill is an ASA Senior Coach and has worked with the national squad for the last 8 years. He was with the England team at the 1990 Commonwealth Games in New Zealand.

Colin Hardy

Colin has been associated with swimming both as a competitor and teacher/coach for many years. He is currently a lecturer in the Department of Physical Education and Sports Science at Loughborough University and is in charge of aquatics. He is also coach to the University swimming team. He has been involved in the training of teachers of Physical Education since 1964, and has written numerous articles for academic and professional journals. He has also written three books on swimming, the most recent of which is *Swimming for Health*. He has also contributed to several other major publications on Physical Education and swimming. He is an ASA Senior Tutor and an RLSS Examiner as well as also being a current Masters champion.

Joan Harrison

Joan is an ASA Principal Tutor and tutors courses for teachers of swimming, diving, synchronised swimming, aquafit, parent and child and for teachers of people with disabilities. Joan was formerly Head of Physical Education and Creative Studies at Sunderland Polytechnic and has a wide range of interests across the whole field of Physical education and Dance. She is also a member of the ASA Education Committee.

Lynn Hogarth

Lynn was originally a competitive swimmer who retired at 19 and began taking an interest in teaching and coaching. In 1986 she became Chief Coach to the Hull Masters Swimming Club and in 1988 she became Swimming Co-ordinator for Hull City Council. She is currently Swimming Development Officer/Coach for Cambridge City Council. Lynn is an ASA Coach as well as a Preliminary Tutor for both the teaching and coaching certificates. She also tutors Assistant Club Coach Certificate courses.

Tony Holmyard

Tony trained at Loughborough and taught Physical Education in Bristol for 6 years. He was for 2 years an ASA National Technical Officer before taking up his current post as a lecturer in the Physical Education Department of Bristol University. His interests include swimming, health related fitness and the acquisition of skill. He is an ASA Coach and Advanced Teacher, and is an ASA Principal Tutor (Teaching) and Senior Tutor (Coaching). Tony is a member of several ASA committees. He is also a very active Masters swimmer and veteran water polo player.

Colin Lee

Former competitive swimmer and water polo player and has taught swimming for some 25 years. Colin trained as a teacher of Physical education at Goldsmiths' College, later gained his B.Ed degree at St Pauls College, Cheltenham, and his Ph.D at the University of London. He taught for 10 years in primary schools in London and Bath and is currently Head of Physical Education at Bath College of Higher Education. Colin has carried out extensive research into skill acquisition by young children, and lectures to several major organisations on this topic.

Mike Seddon

Mike is a Senior Lecturer in Sports Studies at Liverpool Institute of Higher Education and has a special interest in swimming and community health. He is a Moderator and Trainer of Tutors for the Health Education Authority within the *Look after Your Heart: Look After Yourself* programme, and has a strong belief in the value of swimming as a lifetime activity. He is also an ASA Principal Tutor.

Nick Sellwood

After gaining his B.Ed degree at the College of St Paul and St Mary, Cheltenham, where he specialised in Physical Education, Nick taught for 4 years. He was Assistant Swimming Management Officer for Birmingham City Council for 2 years and is currently Director of Swimming for City of Coventry Swimming Club. He has a wide range of coaching experience, including being coach to the England Esso Youth Squad.

David Sparkes

David is an engineer by training and is Managing Director of a small engineering business in the West Midlands. His swimming career was based on a small club in Worcestershire. He is an ASA Principal Tutor and an ASA Coach. He is currently Chairman of the ASA Education Committee as well as serving on the ASA Management Committee and ASA Committee.

Trevor Thomas

Trevor became involved in swimming as a parent in 1955, and embarked on the usual teacher/coach qualification "treadmill". He is active in teaching/coaching and administration, as well as being Team Manager to various England swimming teams, including the 1986 Commonwealth Games. Trevor is an ASA Tutor and Principal Tutor, has served on Education Committees from Club level to ASA Education Committee and has also served on the Visual Aids and Publications Working Party, in which capacity he was jointly responsible for the detailed production of several reprints of *The Teaching of Swimming* publication. He is a tutor/examiner of ASA Swimming Officials, a FINA list referee and starter, officiating at all levels, including the European Championships and the Seoul Olympic Games. President of the ASA in 1988.